PRAISE FOR *CREATE A THRIVING FAMILY LEGACY*

"Do you want to transfer wealth in a way that doesn't ruin your children or grandchildren? Do you want to transfer your values, not just your valuables, and build a Thriving Family Legacy that can last for generations to come ... and even for eternity? I highly recommend reading Create a Thriving Family Legacy: How to Share your Wisdom and Wealth with Your Children and Grandchildren. *I've known the author, Jeff Rogers, for over twenty-five years and he is a thought leader in helping families to create plans that combine both effective wealth transfer and intentional wisdom transfer."*

—Howard Dayton

Founder, Compass—Finances God's Way

Author, Money & Marriage God's Way *and* Charting Your Legacy

"Wisdom transfer as well as wealth transfer—what an idea! Jeff dives through a comprehensive approach for making sure your intentions and money say the same thing. Create a Thriving Family Legacy: How to Share your Wisdom and Wealth with Your Children and Grandchildren *combines field-tested advice, practical suggestions, and biblical wisdom for families that have been entrusted with much."*

—Todd DeKruyter

President, Family Meridian

Author, Navigating Life with More Than Enough

"Rare are the books that contain equal portions of wisdom and technical expertise. There is a difference between the two, as you well know, and both are essential for today and for the future generations of your family. Jeff Rogers delivers both in this readable book—just as he has been delivering both to over one hundred families through his practice over the last thirty-five years."

—Jeff Spadafora

Founder and President, The Way

Former Director, Global Coaching Services and Product Development, Halftime

Author, The Joy Model: A Step-by-Step Guide to Peace, Purpose, and Balance

"Anyone seeking to prioritize passing wisdom along with wealth would benefit from reading this book. Jeff is experienced, competent, and passionate about assisting families to live into and pass along a godly legacy. I couldn't agree more with Jeff's invitation and challenge to be intentional about the legacy you are leaving!"

—Todd Harper

President, Generous Giving

"*Jeff has a unique gift for bringing transformational clarity and wisdom to the estate and legacy planning process.* Create a Thriving Family Legacy *provides a roadmap and great insight into what can be accomplished (but seldom is through traditional planning) in leaving an intentional, strategic, and lasting legacy. This book is a must read for those that want to steward all of the 'wealth' God has entrusted to them—not only their financial resources, but also their time, talents, relationships, and influence to build a thriving and lasting family legacy.*"

—Michael King, J.D.

Vice President and Gift Planning Attorney, National Christian Foundation

"*In his book,* Create a Thriving Family Legacy: How to Share your Wisdom and Wealth with Your Children and Grandchildren, *Jeff Rogers shares, 'Everyone ... will leave a legacy ... intentional or unintentional ... well-planned or unplanned.' These words could not be more true. Being well planned results in wisdom; wisdom brings peace and peace within a family is as rare as it is valuable. What Jeff brings to the reader of this book is how to transfer wisdom along with wealth. Without the former, the latter will dissipate and peace will disappear. The stakes are extremely high and those who have been blessed with wealth or who may receive it would do well to spend time with this book ... not just read it ... spend time with it.*"

—David H Wills, JD

President Emeritus, National Christian Foundation

"Create a Thriving Family Legacy *offers practical, biblical wisdom for anyone grappling with issues of wealth and family. Through storytelling and insightful commentary, the book encourages families to carefully consider the inheritance they give their children and to pass on wisdom along with wealth."*

—Bill High

CEO, The Signatry: A Global Christian Foundation

Author, Giving It All Away … And Getting It All Back Again: The Way of Living Generously

CREATE A THRIVING FAMILY LEGACY

CREATE A

HOW TO SHARE YOUR WISDOM AND WEALTH

THRIVING

WITH YOUR CHILDREN AND GRANDCHILDREN

FAMILY LEGACY

JEFF ROGERS

ForbesBooks

Published by ForbesBooks, Charleston, South Carolina.
Member of Advantage Media Group.

ForbesBooks is a registered trademark, and the ForbesBooks colophon is a trademark of Forbes Media, LLC.

Printed in the United States of America.

10 9 8 7 6 5 4 3 2 1

ISBN: 978-1-946633-04-0
LCCN: 018958850

Cover design by Melanie Cloth.
Layout design by Megan Elger.

This publication is designed to provide accurate and authoritative information in regard to the subject matter covered. It is sold with the understanding that the publisher is not engaged in rendering legal, accounting, or other professional services. If legal advice or other expert assistance is required, the services of a competent professional person should be sought.

Advantage Media Group is proud to be a part of the Tree Neutral® program. Tree Neutral offsets the number of trees consumed in the production and printing of this book by taking proactive steps such as planting trees in direct proportion to the number of trees used to print books. To learn more about Tree Neutral, please visit **www.treeneutral.com**.

Since 1917, the Forbes mission has remained constant. Global Champions of Entrepreneurial Capitalism. ForbesBooks exists to further that aim by bringing the Stories, Passion, and Knowledge of top thought leaders to the forefront. ForbesBooks brings you The Best in Business. To be considered for publication, please visit **www.forbesbooks.com**.

To Gram Rogers, Dad and Mom, and Jesus Christ.
And to the numerous mentors and other influencers in my life
who made this book possible.

TABLE OF CONTENTS

SECTION ONE: PERSONAL LEGACY

SECTION TWO: FAMILY LEGACY

SECTION THREE: FINANCIAL LEGACY

FOREWORD

Jeff Rogers titles the introduction to his new book, *Create a Thriving Family Legacy,* "The Wealthy and The Wise." This is both a great promise and a great summary of the book! Those two words do not always go together in real life. I have had the privilege of being in the financial services world serving literally thousands of people for over fifty years. For the last forty of those years, I have worked almost exclusively in the Christian world helping families plan and manage their finances. I have concluded that there are three questions that we all need to answer relating to our finances. First, who owns it? Second, how much is enough? Third, is the next steward chosen and prepared to receive the God-given financial resources entrusted to me? I have found that many have dealt with the first question, but few have dealt with the second and third questions.

Most Christians say they believe that God owns it all, but rarely do I find that people have set finish lines on either the wealth they accumulate or the amount they should plan to pass to their heirs. Compounding this problem is that the third stewardship question is rarely ever addressed or addressed with faulty information or false assumptions. If I really believe that God owns it all, that makes me a steward of His resources and the last stewardship decision that I must make is who will steward the resources God entrusted to me for His glory.

I have known and worked with Jeff Rogers for many years and know that he unequivocally follows some principles on the wealth transfer question in which I believe strongly and have even written about in a book I published several years ago called *Splitting Heirs*. First of all, I believe that passing wealth without having already passed wisdom is a formula for tragedy. Wisdom may help to create wealth, but wealth is never guaranteed to create wisdom.

Secondly, every person passing wealth should be asking how that wealth will impact the recipient's life, marriage, and children. The last thing that a parent wants to do is to damage their children and/or their families by giving them wealth that they are unprepared to steward. God treats each one of us uniquely because we are unique creations. Yet when it comes to wealth transfer to multiple heirs, most people treat everyone equally.

Thirdly, it has been my experience that husbands and wives many times have widely differing opinions on who should get what. As my mentor, Dr. Howard Hendricks, said, "God did not give you a spouse to frustrate you, but to complete you." In other words, husbands and wives need to process together and come to "their" decision, not "his" or "hers."

Another major mistake that I see in transferring wealth is that people start the wealth transfer process by looking at the tools and techniques of estate planning when in fact the tools and techniques should only be a result of the estate planning process and accomplish the real objectives of the one who is passing the wealth.

Finally, a family meeting is essential, but rarely happens. I used to tell my clients that a family meeting will happen either at your initiative or in the attorney's office after the funeral. It would be best that they hear your values and desires from you directly. By not having a family meeting, you run the risk of creating a "coping gap" when the estate is distributed. A coping gap is when expectations do not meet reality. This will almost always result in disillusionment, anger, and disappointment occurring with no way for you to do anything about it.

The hallmark of this book is biblically based intentionality of the wealth transfer decision combined with intentional wisdom transfer. Jeff has written a book based upon many years of experience that is sound and drips with wisdom. It is a privilege for me to write the foreword of a book that I pray gets wide distribution, as it is so practical and covers so many differing situations.

—Ron Blue
Founding Director, Kingdom Advisors
Author, *Splitting Heirs, Master Your Money and Wealth to Last*

ACKNOWLEDGMENTS

Gram Rogers, thank you for giving me my first Bible, for sharing God's word and His love with me. Thank you for the godly example and legacy of sacrificial generosity you lived out before me. You inspired me, Gram! The seeds you planted in my life are bearing great fruit for God's glory! I know you are looking down from heaven, smiling, and still praying for me.

Dad and Mom, thank you for raising Elaine, Brian, and me with strong family values. You both worked hard, sometimes two to three jobs, to provide a better life for us than what you both grew up with … and you succeeded! Dad, you were an encouraging example of how a husband should love and adore his wife. I am grateful for the virtues and character you instilled within us, including making us work and learn the value of a dollar. I didn't appreciate it then, but I look back now and know those were valuable lessons of wisdom you taught me. Most of all, I am thankful for the persistent love you always showed me (even during my juvenile delinquent years!) Your love was unconditional and for that I am grateful! I love you, Dad!

Dann Harris, God used you to change the trajectory of my life! You recognized God's call on my life and His giftedness and you inspired and challenged me to pursue it heartily and with passion for His glory. You went from being my boss to being my best friend and my primary business and spiritual mentor. I have been blessed to have a number of good mentors and people who have discipled me over my life, but none have had a more significant and transformational influence on my life than you. I love you, Dann!

Howard Dayton, I remember the day we met in your office at Crown Oak Center. From my first Crown study (and the dozens of Crown and Compass—Finances God's Way studies since then), God has used you to transform my view of finances and stewardship. It is through your writings and influence that I first learned God's financial principles. Having violated them in my early adult years, I needed to apply them to "dig out" from the financial pit I had dug. In doing so, we went from financial bondage to financial freedom. By living His principles I've had "Freedom to Live, Freedom to Give, and Freedom to Serve." I have learned so much from you that it would take this entire book to list them all. I quote you often throughout this book. More than all the studies you've created or the teaching you've done, your biggest influence has been because I've seen you live out God's principles sometimes through difficult circumstances, but always with humility, faithfulness, and grace! The way you served your wife, Bev, through the last several years of her life while battling with cancer is truly inspiring! Your message to husbands to "View every request from your wife as an opportunity to serve her" and the way you lived that out is the best example I've ever seen of Ephesians 5:25 (NIV); "Husbands, love your wives, just as Christ loved the church and gave himself up for her." You are the real deal, my friend! Thank you for being my friend and mentor over so many years! Only eternity will reveal the impact of your life … and it will! I love you, Howard!

Ron Blue, thank you for your friendship and faithfulness over so many years! God has used your leadership in numerous ministries (Campus Crusade for Christ—Cru, Crown, Walk through the Bible, etc.). He has also used your numerous books and messages to challenge and inspire millions as you challenged them to "Master Your Money" and develop a plan for financial freedom. I first took Master Your Money back when it was on VHS! It helped shape my Biblical understanding of stewardship and God's financial principles. I am so thankful that you took Larry Burkett's challenge to prayerfully consider taking over the leadership of what is now Kingdom Advisors! God has used your leadership and influence to not only impact my life but the lives of several thousand Kingdom Advisor members who are no longer "Christians who are financial advisors," but now are truly "Christian financial advisors" (or growing to become one). Not a business day goes by that I don't share with clients or other advisors one of the many principles I've learned from you (Six Transcendent Financial Principles, Five Uses of Money (now four), Eleven Buckets, etc. The two I use the most are: "We need to love our children equally but treat them uniquely" (from your book *Splitting Heirs*) and "We need to turn DOWN the static of this world and turn UP the volume of God's word" (from your book *Surviving Financial Meltdown*). I'm convinced the latter, although one of your lesser-known quotes, is the key to people finding contentment in the midst of a "noisy" world. I quote you often throughout this book. God also used you to give me the most humbling experience of my life when you and Kingdom Advisors honored me with the Larry Burkett Award. As you read the characteristics of what Larry looked for in a financial advisor, I was so humbled! Normally I'm pretty confident even in front of large groups, but I lost it and wept like a baby in front of 1,000 other Kingdom Advisors! Ron, thank you for your friendship, your faithful leadership and for your influence on my life! I love you, Ron!

Ray Lyne, the "Grandfather of Christian Estate Design," thank you for your friendship and being a mentor in my life! God has used you greatly in your work with scores of ministries to help release an untold amount of Kingdom Capital to help fulfill the Great Commission (or as you like to say to "Fund the Evangel"). My understanding of Biblical stewardship and estate design has been radically transformed by your influence. There are hundreds of waitresses and servers in restaurants and hotel housekeeping staff that should be grateful to you because you challenged us to see "tipping" as a modern form of the "gleaning fields" and a way that we can bless and serve those who serve us and who are often struggling to make a living and provide a better life for their family. I am a more generous tipper because of you! I quote you often throughout this book and quote you almost every time I do a seminar or workshop or in many meetings with clients. Your "Three Hugs" analogy transformed my paradigm and my life. Every day I try to live intentionally for those "Three Hugs" and I try to inspire and challenge others to live their lives and design their estate and legacy plans in pursuit of the "Three Hugs." Thanks for your friendship, Ray, and for the influence you've had on my life and hundreds of others involved in "Funding the Evangel." I love you, Ray!

Cathy, they say that behind every good man is a great woman, and that is certainly true of me. You have given me the freedom to pursue the calling God put on my life. You've supported the long hours that I work, you have packed untold suitcases so I could travel to serve clients and God's Kingdom (and you have packing down to a science; if anybody deserves a PhD in packing, it's you! You have been a "keeper of the home," a colleague in the business, and an example of the "Helper/Help-mate" that the Bible talks about. What I'm especially grateful for is how you've served your Dad over the last five years, and my Dad over the last two years, as we have served as caregivers for them in our home with you serving as primary caregiver. I told Howard Dayton a few years ago that one of my joys as a husband is seeing how you serve your Dad ... and knowing that if I ever need care, that's the kind of loving care I'm going to receive! Wow! You get the Daughter and Daughter-in-Law Award! I thank God for blessing me with a caring and supportive wife and thank you for being my helper, my friend, and my wife! I love you, Cathy!

Lord Jesus, thank you for your incomprehensible love, your grace, and your mercy! Without you, this book, my life, and my very existence would not be possible! Thank you for being the ultimate example of "family sacrifice." You have modeled out the ultimate "Family Legacy" with millions of "children," like me, who you adopted into your family. You are the Owner of all and we are your stewards. May you use this book to help families steward well all that you've entrusted to them. You are the creator of all wealth and all wisdom. Help all who read this book to create an effective plan for transferring wealth and an intentional plan for transferring your wisdom and values to their children and grandchildren as part of their family legacy. Lord, I feel so blessed to have enjoyed a business and career that is also a ministry and a calling. So few people have that sense of passion and inspiration about what they do for a living. Lord, nothing good happens apart from you, so I pray that as each reader reads this book, they will hear you speaking to them, challenging them, inspiring them, encouraging them to live their lives in such a way as to hear "Well done, my good and faithful servant! You have been faithful with a few things; I will put you in charge of many things. Come and share your master's happiness!"

A WORD FROM THE AUTHOR

Of the few books on family legacy, even fewer are written from a faith-based perspective. Imagine a world in which families build for eternity with God's word as the basis for their stewardship. To encourage that growth is the goal of Stewardship Legacy Coaching™.

I am a Christian, and that faith is at the core of who I am. This book, though intended primarily for Christian families and business owners, is not exclusively for them. I am confident that those who do not share my faith perspective—and that includes some of my clients—will find here a compelling strategy for leaving a lasting family legacy. As an ambassador for my faith, I will be true to my heart as I share my story.

Everyone of any faith, or lack of faith, will leave a legacy, whether good or bad, intentional or unintentional, well-planned or unplanned.

> Everyone will leave a legacy ... what will be yours, and how long will it last?

What will be yours, and how long will it last? In many families, the legacy ripples through a few decades at most. Other families, unwilling to accept a mere ripple, anticipate that their legacy will sweep like a tsunami through generation after generation. They want a legacy that will last for eternity.

What words would you like to be spoken at your memorial service or to be inscribed on your tombstone? How would you want your children, grandchildren, and great grandchildren to remember you? Imagine that you could write your own legacy. The good news is you can and that's what this book is all about. If you want to find out how to create an intentional plan for a lasting legacy, read on.

The number of financially blessed families in America is increasing as the builder and the baby boomer generations grow older. Many of them are examining what their family legacy will be. The elders need to prepare their heirs to become effective stewards of their inheritance and perhaps to take the reins of a family business. That calls for more than the transfer of wealth. That calls for a transfer of wisdom.

Wisdom is the reflection of virtues and values. Parents and grandparents often are less than thrilled with the directions in which their children or grandchildren are going. They sometimes shake their heads at the lack of character they perceive in the coming generations. Business owners may worry that their founding principles will be forsaken. They want to avoid "mission drift."

Family leaders can take heart in knowing they can do much to foster and instill those virtues and values upon which the family was built. Business owners, as well, can transfer the organization's vision, mission, core values, guiding principles, and culture to those who will carry it forward into a productive future.

You have learned many lessons in your lifetime. Perhaps a wise mentor helped you along, or perhaps you learned through mistakes along the way. The question now is whether you have an intentional and proactive plan to take those life lessons and that wisdom and pass it on to your children, grandchildren, great grandchildren, or throughout your business.

Stewardship Legacy Coaching differs from traditional estate planning, which involves merely the transfer of wealth with the aim of leaving the maximum amount of it to the next generation. Traditional planning is about preparing the wealth for the heirs. Our emphasis, by contrast, is about preparing the heirs for the wealth. It is as much about passing on values as it is about passing on valuables. It is as much about passing on wisdom as it is about passing on wealth—perhaps more so.

I hope to inspire you with a new approach to building a family legacy that will endure for generations. We will be considering much more than your money and your stuff. The wealth transfer is certainly important, and we will be examining the legal, tax, financial, and technical aspects of building a strong family legacy. We will be doing so, however, in the context of wisdom transfer. Without the latter, what is the point of the former?

A glance at the table of contents will show you how this book is structured. You will see five sections that reflect the five major areas that we consider to be whole life stewardship. We will look at the personal, family, financial, business, and Kingdom aspects of legacy that together create a holistic approach to stewardship. Each of the sections has two chapters, with the themes generally organized into the issues of wisdom transfer and wealth transfer, although those discussions, by their nature, will overlap.

> We will look at the personal, family, financial, business, and Kingdom aspects of legacy that together create a holistic approach to stewardship.

We begin with the need to identify purpose and passion in one's personal life. Why were you put here on this earth at this time in history? What is the mark that you are meant to leave? How will the lives of your children and grandchildren be different because of you? Will the world be a better place because you were here? Will you leave an impact on eternity?

Will the world be a better place because you were here?

In this book, you will see that I believe it is my calling and my ministry to help families build strong and lasting legacies. I will share with you my own story that led to that calling, in which I now have been engaged for over thirty years. It is my privilege to show families how they can generously release resources that will further God's Kingdom and support the causes that are near and dear to their hearts. This is my passion. It is what drives me.

We are accomplishing much more than just showing financially blessed people how they can give more to charity or just build "bigger barns." We are showing them how to build strong families of enduring character. I wish to serve and guide them, doing my part not only to strengthen families, but also to spread God's word and help to fulfill the Great Commission throughout the earth. I have messages God has put in my heart. Come along with me, in the chapters ahead, as I share them.

—Jeff Rogers

INTRODUCTION

THE WEALTHY AND THE WISE

Wisdom along with an inheritance is good.
… For wisdom is protection just as money is protection.

—Ecclesiastes 7:11–12 (NASB)

Inside the front cover of the Bibles that my grandmother gave my brother and me when I was ten, she wrote, "Read Psalm 46:1." This was a birthday present, but it was not my birthday, nor was it my brother's. It was hers. That's the way Gram Rogers was. She was generous. Others receive gifts on their birthday, but Gram gave us a gift that would change our lives and our eternal destinies.

"God is our refuge and strength, a very present help in trouble" were the words I saw when I turned to that verse. Gram Rogers knew so well what I needed, though I didn't have a clue myself, and I wouldn't discern the truth for several years. Gram had prayed that I would find the way on my spiritual journey, but I was far from it.

By age thirteen, I had become a juvenile delinquent in our rural New Hampshire town. My parents thought I was a good kid—and at home, I was. Outside the house, I not only hung out with the wrong crowd but was a leader of that crowd. The details are unimportant. To describe my wrongdoing would only glorify it. Suffice it to say that I made life miserable for my teachers, my classmates, the police … and I found that the "high" of fighting and drinking and evil mischief doesn't last. There are consequences to the choices we make in life, and I was about to discover them.

But then God, in His divine grace and mercy, drew me to Himself.

SEEDS TAKING ROOT

The seeds had been planted years earlier. From as early as I can remember, Gram shared her faith, not only in words but through the example of her life and her actions. I would tag along as she visited people in need, sharing the joy of Christ as she brought them groceries and other necessities. For years she sold real estate and Avon and was successful. With that sales ability she probably could have been rich in this world's goods, but she chose to be poor as she met the needs of others. She gave away much of her money. She lived out her faith as a model of joy and generosity.

Gram had a radiant smile and, with her red hair before it turned gray, she looked somewhat like Lucille Ball. Though she knew the source of joy, there were earlier times in Gram's life when she wasn't smiling as much. The Great Depression had been difficult enough, but she also had married a mean man who beat their children, one of whom was my father, who left home at age twelve to get away from the abuse. One of my aunts took such severe beatings that she was emotionally troubled all her life. Gram tried to protect her children, stepping in at times to stop her husband, and he would turn his wrath and his fists against her.

Despite his ill temper, my grandfather professed to be a religious man, and he was the son of a minister who also beat his children. In fact, my father said the two of them were the meanest men he had ever known. It was because of my father's bad experience with religion as a boy that he was not eager to become a Christian himself. My mother, too, was raised in a strict and harsh religious atmosphere that made her wary of church. That is why I did not have the privilege of growing up in a Christian family. My mother and father did teach us honesty, patriotism, and a strong work ethic. They were great parents in that way, but they didn't teach me about Jesus Christ because they didn't know Him.

Nonetheless, because of Gram's example I had an innate knowledge of God. I believed that He was who He said He was, and that the Bible was the true word of God and that Jesus was His son. Once, during sixth-grade biology class, I spoke out boldly against the theory of evolution by presenting the facts of creation. Even as an unsaved teen on a troubled path, I knew about Christ, though I didn't know Him as my personal Savior. Even as I was going astray in my junior high years, I still embraced the truth. I was living a double life, and it seemed something would have to give.

It did. About that time, my best friend's mother started a youth group in the church of our small town. My friend, and partner in evil, had no choice but to attend, After all, his mother was leading the group. He had grown up in a Christian home. His father had been a police officer who found the Lord and decided to become a pastor, but then died in a car crash. My friend was just a little boy at the time, and his loss caused him to go astray. Nonetheless, he grew up in and around the church, with a mother who modeled the Christian life. As for me, I accompanied him to the youth group because he was my best friend, and because they did fun things such as bowling and roller-skating.

It was there that I first heard the plan of salvation; the good news of Jesus Christ and His loving sacrifice for me. I heard about his death, burial, and resurrection—for me! I learned that I would have to give an account one day to God for my actions. I knew that I needed Jesus Christ in my life. My daddy didn't raise no fool! I could fool my parents and the teachers and the police, but I knew that I couldn't fool almighty God.

One night at a youth rally attended by hundreds, I saw the reality of heaven and hell. I saw how far short I was falling from God's standards. The seeds that my grandmother had planted finally took root in me. She had shown me the joy of Christ and the example of generosity, but never had I confronted the consequences of my sinfulness. I knew that as things stood, I wasn't on the side of righteousness, and that would mean eternity in hell. That night, I became a Christian.

My life radically changed almost overnight. No longer did I feel proud to be bad. My best friend, too, got right with Christ that night. The two of us ceased to be leaders for evil in our junior high school and started to become leaders for good. The old things passed away. We began growing in Christ.

It was as if a revival were taking place in our school. Many young people came to know Christ. We began having fellowship with teachers who we hadn't known were Christians. Our school was experiencing a transformation, and I was eager to play an active role in doing God's work. Another young man who had been a leader in our group also turned his life around. Instead of hating people, we started loving people. Instead of hurting them, we began helping them.

Soon I was also seeing God at work in the lives of the rest of my family. The pastor of the church where I went to the youth group was also my school bus driver. Mel Jones was probably the friendliest man I have ever met, forever smiling and offering enthusiastic handshakes. After I began attending church, he would visit our home, and in his winsome way he befriended my mother and father. He heard the story of why they had turned their backs on religion, and he gently answered their every question and objection.

As I continued to grow in Christ, I wanted to be baptized, and my family came out to share that celebration with me at a little lake in New Hampshire. There, as the pastor proclaimed the Gospel, my brother, Brian, stepped forward. He became a Christian that day. About a year later, my dad became a believer at an evangelistic service at our church, and at a service a year after that, my mom became a believer as well. One Christmas, we decided to buy a new Bible for my other grandmother, Gram Humphrey. The family asked me to write a personal note in it, expressing our love for her and sharing the plan of salvation. Within months, she surrendered her life to the Savior.

"Believe in the Lord Jesus Christ," the Bible tells us in Acts 16:31 (NHEB), "and thou shalt be saved, and thy house." I was watching that truth in action. Though that verse was directed to the centurion, I had taken it as a promise and prayed that God would save my entire household—and He did!

"YOU NEED TO COME HOME ..."

A few years later, as I was graduating from high school and determining what I would do next, I decided to go into vocational ministry. I went to Word of Life Bible Institute in Schroon Lake, New York, and was planning to go on to Liberty University and Dallas Theological Seminary. I thought that was God's will for me, and I had it all mapped out. Then one day, as graduation was approaching at Word of Life, I was talking on the phone with my father back in New Hampshire.

"Jeff, I don't know why, but I really feel like you need to come back to New Hampshire," he told me. I paused, taking in his words.

"Dad, there are no Christian colleges or seminaries in New Hampshire," I pointed out.

"I know. I just feel that way," he said. "I'm not demanding it. I'm not telling you what to do, but it's this strong feeling that I have."

He was my father, and I felt that I needed to honor his counsel even though it made no sense to me. I returned to our home in New Hampshire and got a job, and I became involved both in high school youth ministry and in college and career ministry. At night I took courses at a local business college, and I listened for God's direction. It was 1981, and I was young with so many years ahead of me.

One morning, a few months after my return, as I was brushing my teeth, I heard a noise from my parents' bedroom. My dad was in the kitchen preparing for his day, and he also heard the sound.

"Boys, are you all right? Was that you?" he called out.

"No," we answered in unison, and the three of us already were rushing to check on my mom. What we had heard, I believe, was the guttural exhalation that some people call the death cough, the sound of life leaving a body. That, at least, was how it seemed to me.

Mom was gone. I knew that, even as I rushed to dial for help from the head of our youth group, one of the state's top paramedics. He arrived within minutes. Meanwhile my brother, an emergency medical technician, tried to revive her. Their efforts were for naught. Mom had had a massive heart attack.

Even as grief gripped my heart, I felt a deep peace settling in alongside it. I had lost my mother, but I knew without a doubt that she was in the presence of Jesus. And I also knew then the first reason that God had redirected my path back to New Hampshire. He wanted me to be there on that day. Though my father and brother were Christians, they still were relatively young in their faith. In a way I served as the family's spiritual leader, offering support and strength in that difficult time.

At my mom's funeral, I had the opportunity to share the Gospel and the blessed assurance of believers that our loved ones who know Christ are with Him in heaven and that one day we will be reunited with them. My oldest sister reached out for the Lord at the funeral, and it was my best friend's mother, the woman who had started the youth group, who led her in prayer. My thoughts turned again to Acts 16:31. I had believed in Christ, and my entire immediate family had come to faith in Him.

Now let's fast-forward a year or so, when the day came that my father married the widow who had started the youth group where I found my salvation. In God's divine sense of humor, my spiritual mom became my stepmom, and my best friend became my stepbrother as well as my brother in Christ.

> In God's divine sense of humor, my spiritual mom became my stepmom, and my best friend became my stepbrother as well as my brother in Christ.

Such is what God can do. He can transform families. If your loved ones have yet to take the step of faith, never give up hope. He is still at work. Pray for them and live out your life faithfully in front of them, and God will reach them in His time. I have seen what He has done in my family, and His love can break through to your family as well.

DISCOVERING GOD'S CALLING

God, as it turned out, had other reasons for bringing me home to New Hampshire, as I soon would come to see. His plan for my career was not the one that I had envisioned. As I was working and getting involved in youth ministry, another good friend introduced me to a company called Christian Mutual Life, whose motto was "Serving the Savior and the Saved." Founded in 1885, it had long helped Christians and churches to be good stewards of what God had entrusted to them.

I joined Christian Mutual Life in 1983, a couple years after my mother's death. What attracted me to the company was the uniqueness of its ministry. It was committed to not investing any of the clients' money in companies involved in abortion or pornography, gambling or other things that ruin peoples lives, lead to bondage, and destroy families. Instead, it helped fund the building of Bible-preaching churches, Christian schools, and camps around the country.

I was excited about that mission. I liked the combination of helping people to be wise stewards while using the money for good and furthering the Great Commission.

God poured out His blessings. I was the rising young star in the company and soon became a manager and within a few years, a regional vice president. And along the way, I fell in love. My manager had asked me to join him in southern New Hampshire and help him open a Massachusetts office. While I was there, I attended his church. And there I met Cathy. Her mother ran the nursery, and her father played piano and was a church leader. Cathy had been in that church since she was in the womb. When I met her as a young woman, still in her teens, I appreciated both her outer and inner beauty. She already was deeply involved in ministry. We went out on a date, and another, and a few years later, in 1986, I asked Cathy to marry me.

That was about the same time that the company asked me to open a new location, agreeing to wait until after the wedding. I was given great leeway on where in the country I would open this new office, with only a few exceptions. It was still a relatively small company, with lots of wide-open space where we could set new roots. Cathy and I prayed on it. We looked at the weather map and the demographic maps. And we chose Orlando. Immediately after our honeymoon, we headed to Florida.

We didn't know a soul there, but God again blessed our efforts. I started from scratch to build the Orlando office, and within a year, we were the second-highest-producing branch in the country, superseded only by the branch where I had started with my mentor in New England. In our many years in the Orlando area, Cathy and I have been involved together in a variety of ministries, both in leadership and support roles, ranging from our long-time, small-group Bible study, to youth ministry, to assisting ministries such as Compass—Finances God's Way, Campus Crusade for Christ, Wycliffe Bible Translators, World Help, and scores of churches and other ministries.

A few years after our move to Orlando, another company bought out Christian Mutual Life, and it lost the focus that had drawn me to it. The mission that had meant so much to me was missing. For me, this was the death of a vision. I was at a crossroads, and so I sought the counsel of what I call my spiritual board of directors: my pastor, my father, and a few other business and spiritual mentors. Separately but unanimously, they all said something such as this: "Jeff, God has wired you for this business and ministry. You need to find a way to stay in it and to make it work. We encourage you to start your own company."

And so I did. In 1992, I launched what today has become Stewardship Advisory Group. Later we started Stewardship Legacy Coaching, which is our family and business legacy coaching company. Over the years, I have had the privilege of personally serving many families and business owners, and of mentoring and discipling other advisors in our firm's offices around the nation.

Other companies that offer similar services are simply making estate planning more palatable for their clients. We strive to be different by incorporating biblical stewardship into our process. We help families pass on both their wealth and their wisdom. We assist them in planning the financial, legal, and tax issues to effectively transfer wealth to the next generations, and at the same time, we help them become more intentional about passing on their virtues, their family values, their faith, and their wisdom. We call it effective Wealth Transfer combined with intentional Wisdom Transfer™.

Before my father suggested I go home to New Hampshire and everything changed, I had thought I would become a pastor or evangelist. My studies were in evangelism, discipleship, and ministry. I believe that God chose me for this work in stewardship and legacy coaching not because of a background in finances, but rather because He knew my heart. He gave me this passion for a reason.

Once I got into this business, I found that all the technical aspects came easily for me, but as a child I didn't dream of someday becoming a family and business or Stewardship Legacy Coach. God directed my life for His purposes. If I had become a pastor, I might have touched, over the course of my ministry, a few thousand lives in a small New Hampshire church. But because of this work that I'm involved in, I've been able to touch hundreds of thousands of lives through the resources released to fund Christian ministries and churches! Wow, humbling!

In my career, I have prayed with clients and led some of them to Christ, although about 90 percent already are Christians. Those who aren't have generally come to us by referral from a good friend or relative who is a Christian. Our values attract them. We have seen many families become wiser stewards, and we have seen them healed from dysfunctions and difficult family dynamics. We have had the joy and the pleasure of helping numerous families and business owners build powerful legacies.

We also have seen a groundswell of what we call Kingdom Capital™, which are current and planned gifts directed to God's Kingdom that have been dedicated to God's work. At this point, the Lord has used us to help raise over $970 million for the cause of Christ. Within a year or two, we hope to break the $1 billion mark for Kingdom Capital, which has been a longtime goal.

For more than three decades now, it has been my privilege to serve the Lord both personally and through my career. Many years ago, one of my mentors pointed out to me that what we were doing was not just a business and not just a ministry. It was a business/ministry. I see it, as well, as my calling from God.

SECTION ONE
PERSONAL LEGACY

5 AREAS OF YOUR LEGACY

PERSONAL	FAMILY	FINANCIAL	BUSINESS	KINGDOM
Legacy	Legacy	Legacy	Legacy	Legacy

CHAPTER 1

ROOTS AND WINGS

*We will not hide these truths from our children; we will
tell the next generation about the glorious deeds of the
LORD, about his power and his mighty wonders.*

—Psalms 78:4 (NLT)

Tom and Jane had reached the point in life when they were pondering
the meaning of it all. The couple had worked hard for years and
deeply appreciated the family and financial blessings that had come
their way. *This is good*, they thought, *but what's next?* They were
not thinking in terms of how to make another million. They were
thinking in terms of eternity.

Both husband and wife had grown up in middle-class America.
Theirs was not a rag-to-riches story, but it was a story of strong values
and entrepreneurial initiative. The Lord had blessed them, and now,
with two preteen children, their thoughts increasingly turned to their
legacy.

As a boy, Tom had shown early ambition, making some money around the neighborhood by shoveling snow and raking leaves. He opened a Christmas tree lot when he was a teenager. That led to other entrepreneurial endeavors with the Boy Scouts and other organizations. He went on to open a business, eventually selling it and getting into other business lines. His financial net worth had risen to $60 million, and then to $80 million. In the previous year alone, he had made about $20 million from the businesses.

Jane had been involved since childhood in ministry work and missions, and she, too, grew up with strong values. Neither she nor her husband had a wealthy background, but as the years went by, the couple reached a state of affluence far beyond what either of their families ever had experienced.

As Christians, Tom and Jane understood the true source of those resources. "What would the Owner (God) of all this have us do with it?" they asked themselves. "How might we give back to our community, and to the world around us, to make the world a better place? How can we invest in something that will last … forever?"

But growing up in such affluence, would their children embrace that work ethic themselves? Would they appreciate the value of a dollar?

As they thought back to their childhoods, they realized how much they appreciated the work ethic and values that their parents had instilled in them. And certainly, they were teaching their own children, a boy and a girl on the cusp of adolescence, the difference between right and wrong. But growing up in such affluence, would their children embrace that work ethic themselves?

Would they appreciate the value of a dollar? They stood to inherit a fortune someday. Would they be prepared to be good stewards of it?

The couple knew that a good education and a solid moral foundation were essential for success in life, but they realized that their words alone and even their example would fall short of what their children needed. They wanted them to have experiences that would plant those virtues and values deeply in their hearts. It was for this reason that a friend and mentor of the couple introduced them to me and our Stewardship Legacy Coaching process. They decided that our process was exactly what their family needed and engaged us to help them navigate these important issues.

It was an honor to see the transformation that happened as we designed an intentional plan to build an enduring family legacy. With our encouragement, Tom and Jane and their children took steps that changed their lives. Those steps differ for every family with which we work. The strategy is not prescriptive. The best course of action will depend on the family's unique needs and goals. For this family, the transformation began with two mission trips.

The first was an extended stay in Africa with a Christian ministry dedicated to fighting hunger, poverty, and disease while sharing the good news of Jesus Christ. The ministry's focus is to meet not only the practical and material needs of the people but also their emotional and spiritual needs. It strives for a transformational impact, and that often is what happens in the lives of the givers as well as the receivers.

Tom and Jane and, more importantly, their children witnessed a level of poverty there that they never had seen before. They saw desperately hurting people, and it broke their hearts. Later the family took another trip, this time with a mission organization working in the Appalachian Mountains to help people in need. They had not realized the extent of suffering in their own country. To see such impoverishment of body and spirit was both distressing and motivating to them. They wanted to make a difference.

From those experiences, the family gained new perspectives. They have been supporting such ministries generously, helping to adopt a village and sponsoring children and schools. Tom and Jane saw a radical transformation in the lives of their children, who gained a greater appreciation and gratitude for their material and spiritual blessings. Untethered for a time from the Internet and electronics, they found that their games and gadgets held less appeal and that the needs of a hurting world around them were more important than these trivial distractions. The children (and parents) are seeing that their affluence gives them more than the ability to buy things; it gives them the ability to make a difference in the lives of those less fortunate.

> In many wealthy families, the children stand to inherit a fortune, but will they be prepared to wisely handle those resources?

In many wealthy families, the children stand to inherit a fortune, but will they be prepared to wisely handle those resources? In her book *The Golden Ghetto*, Jessie O'Neil defines *affluenza* as "the disease and dysfunction caused by affluence." Many families struggle with children or grandchildren who have an entitlement mentality, slacker syndrome, or "failure to launch"—all of which are the symptoms of affluenza. It doesn't have to be that way. Affluence can open greater opportunities to be a blessing to others when it is combined with wise planning, teaching opportunities, and life-changing experiences. We should use affluence in a positive way to counteract the dysfunctions of affluenza.

The experiences of those mission trips, on which they went without electronic gadgets and saw abject poverty and disease, also strengthened the family bonds between parent and child and brother and sister. Together they felt a depth of thankfulness, and along with that came a keen sense of responsibility for the wealth with which they were entrusted and the blessings that they enjoyed. Their common purpose drew them together in a family spirit of generosity. They felt a responsibility to use their financial blessings and resources to help others less fortunate than themselves here in America and around the world.

The story of this family and their experience is just one example of how to fight back against the risk that affluence might produce in children a sense of entitlement that blinds them to the world's needs. Families of wealth can use their wealth positively, but unless they manage it well, it can also harm them and those around them. You will find that theme woven throughout the pages of this book. Affluence is not wrong, in and of itself. The question is how we steward it, and how we use it. Is the money simply for our own consumption and enjoyment? Or do we generously share with others around us? Is there a purpose to our prosperity?

Is there a purpose to our prosperity?

Much of this book will be about the importance of a family mission to preserve and foster family virtues and values. That mission, however, starts with the individual.

THE SEEDS OF WISDOM

In Tom and Jane's story, we see how a couple took practical actions to galvanize their family to envision a legacy. Much of this book will be about the importance of a family mission to preserve and foster family virtues and values. That mission, however, starts with the individual.

God gives each of us a life purpose, and we each are on our personal path to finding it. We yearn to learn why we are here. In the discovery of our individual missions, we can lead the way for others—in our families, and in our communities—to accomplish what matters most.

Beyond success lies the realm of significance. It's not enough to get to the point of saying, "I've made it," because that raises the sometimes unsettling questions of "Why did I bother?" and "Is this all there is?" The world's definition of success—money, fame, power—fails to satisfy the soul.

Your personal legacy is the key to building a strong family legacy. You can discover your personal legacy by contemplating some fundamental questions. Why were you born into the circumstances in which you find yourself? Why has your life journey been on the path that it has taken? Why are you here, and why does your life matter? It often is not until people's hair is gray, well after they have found worldly success, that they begin seeking God's plan in earnest, asking what they can do that will last.

And thus begins the search for significance. I believe that everyone, ultimately, wants to live a life that matters, that has meaning and significance. The words of Augustine are most appropriate: "Thou hast formed us for Thyself, and our hearts are restless until they find rest in Thee." Or, as Blaise Pascal put it, we mortals try in vain to fill our emptiness, but "This infinite abyss can be filled only with an infinite and immutable object; in other words, by God himself." In other words, all of us have a "God-shaped" hole in our souls that only can be filled by a personal relationship with our Creator!

Our hearts tell us that we were put here for a reason, and in time, our quest for success turns to fulfilling that purpose. We are unlikely to find that fulfillment simply by sitting and pondering the matter. Instead we must be intentional and proactive. I often ask families whether they have a specific plan to mentor and disciple their children and grandchildren—that is, to prepare their heirs by making sure that their wisdom and values are transferred along with their wealth. Most admit they don't have an actual plan for that. They "hope" it will happen. But hope is not a plan!

Money represents our work and our efforts in the world, but when pursued for its own sake, it leads to emptiness. How many times have we seen examples, whether in Hollywood, on Wall Street or Washington, of people who pursued money, fame, and power and, ultimately, found misery? Money, if not wisely stewarded, can harm family relationships. It can squelch initiative and work ethic in the lives of our children and grandchildren. It can create slackers with an entitlement mentality. Rather than empower, it can enable—and disable. However, when we transfer both wisdom and wealth, we empower and prepare our heirs to not just survive, but thrive.

Money's greatest strength is in helping others. It matters most when it is a currency for eternity. Whether wealth becomes a blessing or a curse depends largely on whether it is dispensed along with wisdom. If the rising generations are to have access to that wisdom, it first must be born within the heart of the family leadership. The father and mother, the grandfather and grandmother need to understand what really matters if they are going to build a family legacy. How can the elders expect the youth to carry on values that they themselves have yet to define or expect the younger generation to live with virtues that they themselves are not living out?

Often it is in the heart of grandparents or great-grandparents where great wisdom resides. They may harbor deep concerns about the direction that younger people in the family have been taking. Often, people in their sixties, seventies, or eighties and beyond, are also the ones who are more likely to be thinking about the thriving family legacy.

A legacy, however, is not always something that is passed down to the next generation. Sometimes it is passed UP to the previous one. I am in my early fifties. When I think of my family legacy, my thoughts also turn to how my wife, Cathy, and I might serve our fathers, now that our mothers both have passed on to heaven. These days, people live far longer than once was the case. That presents a great opportunity to reach up to the previous generation, to serve them and love them in their later years, to hear their stories, life lessons, and experiences.

In whichever direction you pass your legacy, if you feel moved to take action, don't wait. Taking action will be your personal legacy.

Each of us will leave one. What will yours look like? Are you sowing the seeds of wisdom into the lives of others so that they might someday bear fruit?

CLARITY OF PURPOSE AND PASSIONS

It's hard to answer such questions when rushing around with all of life's daily responsibilities, but the time comes when we need to hit the pause button and stop long enough to get clarity about our purpose. How do we attain that clarity? Here are some questions to get you started:

- What are the things you are most passionate about? What gets you fired up or brings a smile to your face? What are the things that, when you do them, you feel God's pleasure?

- What are the causes that break your heart? If you could fix one problem in this world, what would it be? If you could relieve one suffering in your community, what would it be?

- What are the causes that you believe break the heart of God? If you could make a difference in those areas and be used for a purpose higher than yourself, what would it be?

The lack of clarity about purpose leads many people to a state of confusion, and they stall out. Instead of moving forward, they don't do anything. Clarity combats that confusion, and it builds confidence that we can fulfill our purpose. And that confidence in itself gives us a greater capacity to do more. Think of it as the four Cs: *Clarity* eliminates *confusion*, which then builds *confidence,* and increases *capacity*.

CLARITY
ELIMINATES
CONFUSION
WHICH BUILDS
CONFIDENCE
AND INCREASES
CAPACITY

Though many people have found financial and business success, they still yearn for significance. How will they leave their mark on this world and on eternity? As has often been observed, people can spend a lifetime climbing the ladder of success, only to find it was leaning against the wrong wall. Sometimes, business people sacrifice their families on the altar of the almighty dollar, missing too many of Johnny's ball games and Suzy's recitals. They and their children look back with regret at the loss, and relationships suffer. The pursuit of success has, in many cases, led to failure in the things that matter most.

Through the Stewardship Legacy Coaching process, we help people to go deeper and gain the clarity that will prevent such regrets. We help them to identify what breaks their own hearts, and what breaks the heart of God. They gain clarity, as well, about their passions.

Those passions often involve noble causes that will impact the world, their communities, and eternity, though often a big step is just to identify something, a hobby, perhaps. That will be a source of great joy and fulfillment. We can help them to see how they might use a hobby in a way that is more than just for recreation and enjoyment. It actually can build the family legacy.

I was talking with a retired client recently who told me he plays golf three times a week, and we looked at ways that he might use that pastime to also pursue a higher purpose. Often, a hobby or sport can be an opportunity to spend some one-on-one time with loved ones, such as a child or grandchild. That time alone with them is precious. Rather than just swatting a golf ball, why not ask what is happening in their lives, what they are dreaming about, what is worrying them? Then, while crossing the fairway, why not look up at the sky and talk about how it all got there? Who created all this? It's an opportunity to build an incredible relationship. It's golf with a higher purpose. Professionals often talk about business deals on the golf course, and that's all well and good, but why not talk about the much bigger deal of life itself?

Many such leisure activities, when shared with others, can deepen the human bond. Whether boating or hiking or enjoying a cup of coffee together, what a beautiful opportunity to get closer to family and friends, or to strengthen a marriage. These are the moments when each of us can share our story and the lessons we have learned on our journey. How natural to do so in the course of having fun. This is a transfer of wisdom, not in a preachy or condescending way, but while just doing life together.

At Stewardship Legacy Coaching, we also help couples to discover, or rediscover, how their passions and purposes line up. Husband and wife, created individually but joined by God as one in marriage, must stand united in defining the family mission. They need to be clear about where they are going and the family legacy that they desire.

On the other side of retirement, after the kids have left home, or after the business is sold, what is next? Many couples lack that clarity. Often, the husband and wife have been on parallel paths. If the wife's identity has been tied up in raising the kids, she now may be wondering what she should be doing now that the nest is empty. Meanwhile, if the husband's identity has been tied up in his career or his business, he may be wondering about his purpose now that he no longer is needed at the office. Their paths have run parallel but separate, and the challenge now is to come together to discover and pursue common purposes and passions.

Stripped of what they thought was their purpose and identity, husbands and wives often feel empty. As a couple, they need to find their common purpose and identity for the second half of their lives. As Bob Buford says in his wonderful, bestselling book *Halftime*: "For the second half of life to be better than the first, you must make the choice to step outside of the safety of living on autopilot. You must wrestle with who you are, why you believe what you profess to believe about your life, and what you do to provide meaning and structure to your daily activities and relationships."

To that end, it is essential that husbands and wives get to know each other again. Divorces among older couples are rampant nowadays. Sometimes they divorce in retirement after spending forty years together. It happens, far too often, after the family business is sold. The couple has all that money from the sale, and they have a lot more time to spend together. But neither knows who the other is. They lack a plan for the second half of their lives. They don't have a purpose together as a couple.

"We've just grown apart," they sometimes try to rationalize. Another way that they could look at it is that they now have an opportunity to grow back together. Rather than each of them venturing out on their own again, they could enter a marvelous growth period in their marriage. It's not enough that they came together and stayed together. Now they must work together. That's success.

It's important that we finish well. Every couple should ask themselves what they can work on together, in the second half of their lives, for personal fulfillment, for the pursuit of passions, and for the family legacy. What virtues and values will they champion as they travel the road together from confusion to clarity, from confidence to capacity? Together they can decide how to have an everlasting impact and serve their family, community, and God.

> Every couple should ask themselves what they can work on together, in the second half of their lives, for personal fulfillment, for the pursuit of passions, and for the family legacy.

INSPIRING THE AMBASSADORS

Most people go through life hoping that the legacy they leave will be a good and lasting one. That is their desire, and the next step is to make it a mission to finish well and leave that kind of legacy. To be good stewards, we must make the most of our time, talents, and treasures to impact the lives of others.

We have so much opportunity to serve God's Kingdom. God puts many people within our sphere of influence, including friends and neighbors and coworkers. We have the ability to touch a multitude of people. It is through our relationships that we expand our ability to serve. Each person whom we touch could in turn become an ambassador who will spread the good news. The essential questions for each of us on our personal journey are these: What are we doing to positively influence others? Are we cultivating relationships to serve eternal purposes?

The first and most important mission field is the family up and down the generations: the children and grandchildren, the parents and grandparents. "You can give your children roots and wings," according to an old saying, "or you can give them money and things." Many people do too much of the latter even though they understand the importance of the former. Children need roots so that they know who they are. They need to know what it means to be part of the family, to be a responsible member of society and to be a patriotic citizen. And they need wings so that they can pursue their destiny and find the purpose for which they were uniquely created.

If you could only give your children or grandchildren roots and wings *or* money and things, which would you give them? The good news is it doesn't have to be a zero-sum game. You can give them both. But I would submit to you that if you give them only money and things—in other words, if you transfer wealth without wisdom—then you will likely harm them. If, however, you give them roots and wings, you will inspire them to greatness (and they can earn their own wealth if they have wisdom).

You can leave a legacy of both wealth and wisdom—that is, if you have attained them both. We should manage our lives so that we are building a personal legacy that is worthy of passing on. As for me, I want my legacy to be this: I was a faithful servant and a good ambassador for Jesus Christ. It's a question that I often ask both individuals and couples: "Are you inspiring your children and grandchildren to become ambassadors as well?"

SHARING YOUR STORY

Each of us has a story. We all can tell tales of life as we knew it when we were growing up, of how things were at home, in school, and with friends. We have memories to share about our first date and our first job, of triumphs and trials, of joys and heartache.

Do your children and your grandchildren know your story? It is an essential element of your family legacy because within it are life lessons that need to be preserved and applied by future generations. Along your journey, through your many experiences, you learned the principles and precepts of your parents and grandparents, and you made choices every step of the way that modeled those values. If you're like me, you also made some mistakes along the way, and because you learned from them, those experiences are important to your story as well. Just as you can show by example what your children and grandchildren should do, you can also show them what they should not do. Share what you've learned from both your mentors and from the school of hard knocks. Your children and grandchildren will learn wisdom from your life lessons and, hopefully, pass them on for generations to come.

Do your children and your grandchildren know your story?

Stories draw families together, and they draw the generations together. Something so valuable merits wise stewardship. What you have put in your memory bank is as important as what you have in your bank account. You need to be intentional about preserving those stories. It happens so often: The elders pass away, and with them go their memories. Their children and grandchildren recall only the outline of the story. They no longer can see the brush strokes that made the portrait of a life so beautiful. Those details were rich in lessons, but they are lost forever. A few generations later, the great grandchildren struggle to remember even the names.

We must share our family stories before it is too late. Tell your loved ones about the twists and turns of life that made you who you are. What does your family represent? What does it mean to be part of your family? Your stories can inspire them to take pride in living up to the family name.

"We will tell the next generation the praiseworthy deeds of the Lord, his power, and the wonders He has done," we are told in Psalms 78:4 (NIV). And Deuteronomy 6:7 (NIV) instructs us to talk to our children about God's ways, "when you sit at home and when you walk along the road, when you lie down and when you get up."

"What's your story about His glory?" the Christian songwriter and artist, Matthew West, asks in his song "Next Thing You Know." Through your own testimony, you have the opportunity to share your faith. You can show how you have strived to live out God's ways, and wherever you fell short you can show how you grew from the incident and experienced God's grace. Your personal legacy is what builds the family legacy. By sharing how you discovered your own roots and wings, you encourage your loved ones to find theirs—and you help to inspire your family's identity and destiny through the generations.

CHAPTER 1 QUESTIONS TO CONSIDER

1. Do your children know your family story and the story of what it was like for you growing up?

2. If you could only pass on one thing to each of your children or grandchildren, what would you pass on to them?

3. If you could give your heirs only one inspirational challenge, word of encouragement, or piece of wisdom, what would you challenge them with?

CHAPTER 2

WISELY STEWARDING YOUR FAMILY WEALTH

Each of you should use whatever gift you have received to serve others, as faithful stewards of God's grace in its various forms.

—1 Peter 4:10 (NIV)

Wisdom does not depend on the size of your portfolio or your net worth. Whether your resources are modest or abundant, your virtues and values should be unchanging as you pass them on. That part of your legacy, which we examined in the last chapter, has nothing to do with money.

Nonetheless, money matters. Your personal wealth is also an essential element of your legacy because of the good that it can do in serving the next generations, your community, the world around you, and the Kingdom of God. Family leaders are called to be good stewards in their financial affairs.

In this chapter, we will look specifically at whom we are best positioned to help accomplish that responsible stewardship and the types of situation in which our clients benefit from our coaching.

More money can lead to more family dysfunction, such as feelings of entitlement and a lack of ambition and motivation—in short, the "affluenza" that can infect loved ones.

That is why "financially blessed" families of relatively high net worth are likely to benefit the most from Stewardship Legacy Coaching. We call them financially blessed out of recognition that wealth and success come from God.

Often people like to think that they are self-made men or women who have pulled themselves up by the proverbial bootstraps. It's a reflection of the common American rags to riches tale and pride in one's ability to overcome. What we must always remember is that it is God who gave us that ability. He gave us the grace. Any opportunities that came our way were because He allowed us to have them. He arranged for them. Deuteronomy 8:18 (NIV) says, "But remember the LORD your God, for it is he who gives you the ability to produce wealth, and so confirms his covenant, which he swore to your ancestors, as it is today."

In other words, there are no self-made people. They just think they are. All our possessions, talents, abilities, and wealth, we owe to God, who deserves the honor and respect as the "ultimate" wealth creator.

In truth, God is the owner of it all. "The earth is the Lord's and everything in it," the Bible says in 1 Corinthians 10:26 (NIV), and that includes us. We are His stewards. We are His managers. He blesses families in many ways, only one of which is financial. When families have built up significant financial resources, however, they need expert guidance in handling that wealth wisely to do good in the world. It should be used to help, not to harm, to empower, not create enablement or entitlement.

THE PEOPLE WE SERVE

Most, though not all, of our clients at Stewardship Legacy Coaching are Christians. They are conservative in their values and beliefs. Many are parents or grandparents who are committed to building a strong family legacy. Some are single, or their spouse has passed on. Some are couples without children and grandchildren but nonetheless place a high value on leaving a lasting legacy.

Many times, those who have begun to think seriously about their personal and family legacy are between the ages of fifty and eighty. That does not mean that younger people do not need to be thinking about their legacy. In fact, they should. The sooner that people get clarity and take definite steps to build a legacy, the better off they will be. They will be way ahead of the game compared with the person who does not get started until age seventy-five.

The clients whom we serve best have a net worth of $10 million or more if they are single, or $20 million or more for married couples. Often they have a significant annual income of $500,000 or more. Many have made their money as business owners, real estate owners, farmers, or ranchers and they want to be a good steward of their business legacy as well as their family legacy.

If bequests are made from the wrong accounts, for example, families can unnecessarily pay hundreds of thousands of dollars in taxes. Let's say a couple has a million-dollar IRA or 401(k)-type retirement account. If the children were to inherit it directly, they would, typically, lose around $400,000 and only get to keep $600,000. If, instead, the children were to receive $1 million of other assets, such as real estate or regular stocks or bonds, they wouldn't pay any income tax on that (because of the step-up in cost basis). They would get to keep the whole million. From a tax perspective, it makes all the difference in the world which assets are left to the children or grandchildren and which assets are left to charity. If a charity inherited that IRA or 401(k), it could keep the entire $1 million because of its tax-exempt status.

Some people have highly appreciated real estate or other investments. They want to avoid the capital gains on their liquidation. Many of our clients also have valuable oil, gas, or other petroleum or mineral assets. The common denominator is that they are at a stage of life where conversion from growth assets to income assets is an attractive proposition for them and they don't want to pay any more taxes than required by law.

In essence, our typical clients are people who have a heart for stewardship and want to be prudent planners. They want to be wise in what they do. They feel a sense of responsibility that comes with their wealth. Often they do want to plan through what I call the **Lens of Biblical Stewardship™**. They are supportive of Christian ministries or other charities and either are already a major donor to a ministry or could become one.

We serve families that desire to create a strong legacy and want to go from success to significance. They are looking to find clarity about their life purpose, and they are committed to finishing well. They want to make a difference in the world. They want to have an impact on eternity.

And they want help along the way. Our clients desire a trusted relationship with a guide who understands both what is in their head and what is in their heart, whether it is for their family or business legacy or for their charitable endeavors. They want a coach who will work collaboratively with their other professionals in shepherding that process, and they are willing to heed the counsel that they get. They have faith in the future, not a fear of it, and don't just want to hear about what they could do. They want to do it.

Not everyone we work with has all those characteristics. In fact, nobody has all those characteristics. That is simply a description of whom we serve best and who might find the Stewardship Legacy Coaching process to be most valuable.

THE THRIVING FAMILY LEGACY ASSESSMENT™

Everyone wants to win. But we want you to win at what matters most. Consider this scorecard of legacy as a tool to help you assess your legacy. It is an assessment by which they can assess how well they are already doing and where they might have gaps. The client ranks a series of statements on a single page from one to five, with one meaning strongly disagree and five meaning strongly agree. I will share some of those here, and you can find a more complete scorecard in the appendix on page 173.

"I/we *can/cannot* clearly envision and communicate the family legacy we would like to create."

"I/we *are/are not* 100 percent confident that all our children and grandchildren would still be 'hugging each other' six months after we died."

"We *have/do not* have a well-defined (and written) Family Vision, Mission, and Core Values Statement."

"All/some of our children or grandchildren *are/are not* fully prepared to be wise stewards of the wealth they might inherit."

"My spouse and I *are/are not* completely in alignment in our vision for our children and grandchildren and our Family Legacy."

"We *do/do not* have an intentional, proactive, and written plan that includes both Wisdom Transfer and Wealth Transfer to our children and grandchildren."

"Both my spouse and I *feel/do not feel* a complete sense of true financial freedom."

"I believe there *are/are not* conflicts and/or unresolved issues in my family that might interfere with building a Thriving Family Legacy."

"I *am/am not* 100 percent sure if we have a Zero Estate and IRD Tax Plan."

SEVEN SIGNIFICANT TRIGGER EVENTS

Major events are a great time to reset, make a tactical change, or move closer to the direction you want. These events trigger great conversations and often are the best time to discuss the issues about legacy. People want to steward these events, which are likely to be the largest financial transactions of their lifetime. It might be a golden parachute and severance package from an employer. It might be the sale of a business that they nurtured for decades. It might be the sale of significant real estate, or other assets. In any case, our clients want to be good stewards of these events.

Once-in-a-lifetime events call for a great degree of wisdom in how they are handled. We have identified seven significant trigger events that the Stewardship Legacy Coaching process helps our clients to manage.

- **The sale, exit, or transition of a business.** We help business owners with their business continuity and succession planning. In the years leading up to that transition, many decisions must be made. Who will take over the business? Will it be someone in the family, perhaps one or more of the children or grandchildren? Have they been properly mentored and trained? Are they fully equipped and empowered to lead and manage the business? What if they are not interested? Might the company be sold to a longtime key employee or team of employees with experience in managing it? Would the best choice be to sell to an outside buyer? We help owners think through those considerations, all the while looking for opportunities to reduce or eliminate the capital gains or income taxes on the sale. A business truly is a stewardship responsibility that goes beyond the financial, legal, and tax issues. It's an opportunity to transfer both wealth and wisdom to the next generation of business stewards and leaders. A business legacy, can endure for generations as a family legacy can—if wisely planned.

- **The sale of real estate**. We can help clients reduce or even eliminate the capital gains tax on the sale of highly appreciated real estate. For example, we recently worked with some people who were selling several million dollars worth of real estate, all of it with a low-cost basis, meaning it had appreciated greatly in value since they had acquired it. If they had just sold it outright, the capital gains taxes would have been staggering. We showed them how to structure the sale with several options to either reduce that tax or eliminate it completely.

- **Excess income over lifestyle**. If you find yourself cringing every time you write one of those quarterly estimated tax checks to the IRS, we can help you lower your income tax and increase the tax efficiency of your investment portfolio as well as your charitable giving. We help with both strategic and tactical tax planning, developing a long-term plan, and annually identifying specific opportunities to save money, from a few thousand dollars to tens of thousands, and even millions, for some clients. Many people are frustrated that their current advisors don't offer them tax-saving suggestions. Their CPAs may be good bookkeepers, accountants, and tax preparers but not as good at tax planning. Many tend to be reactive rather than proactive, telling their clients on April 15 of the next year what they should have done the previous year, *prior to the transaction*! By contrast, our annual Tactical Tax Planning process suggests ideas in time to implement them every year. Although we don't do accounting or tax preparation, we do actively help our clients save significant taxes. We like to work collaboratively with our client's tax professionals, leveraging their expertise and ours proactively.

- **A large taxable estate**. The 2018 federal exemption for estate tax is $11,210,000 per person, or twice that for a married couple. In other words, the value of an estate exceeding that amount is currently subject to a 40 percent federal estate tax. We work with families to reduce or eliminate the amount they must pay. Rarely do our clients, regardless of the amount of their wealth, pay *any* federal estate taxes. We accomplish that through wise planning. We zero out the tax. We do not simply sell them a life insurance policy, as some planners and life insurance agents do. With life insurance, they still are paying the taxes and probably don't like how the government spends all those dollars. Instead, we show our clients legal ways to eliminate the estate taxes. We call that Zero Estate Tax Planning. Many of the wealthiest families in America do not pay a lot in estate taxes because they know the rules, amassing money generation after generation. A leading reason that family businesses, farms, and ranches fail to continue into the next generation is that they must be sold to pay the estate taxes. We help our clients stay fully informed about the rules and know how to wisely navigate them.

- **Large retirement plans.** People who have a lot of money in a retirement plan such as an IRA, 401(k), 403(b), or annuities will face a huge tax on that money when it is transferred to the next generations. That is the IRD tax, which stands for "income in respect of the decedent." Basically, it is the income tax that comes due on tax-deferred investments when left to heirs. The amount of the transfer often is sufficiently large to push the children or grandchildren into the highest marginal tax bracket for the year in which they receive the money. Often they end up paying 37 percent. That's almost 40 percent of your retirement plan that could go to your least favorite governmental agency, the IRS! The IRD Tax is the "gotcha" tax that most Americans don't even know about. We show our clients how to eliminate the IRD tax. Tax-wise giving to charity can be a great saving opportunity.

- **Large amount of corporate stock or options**. Many corporate executives have accumulated stocks or stock options that have greatly appreciated, or upon leaving the company they get a large severance package or the "golden parachute" of a deferred compensation plan. For many of them, this will be the largest financial windfall in their lives, and they must properly steward it. We share strategies to reduce or eliminate the capital gains tax and to lower the income tax. We have saved many clients tens or even hundreds of thousands of dollars on these once-in-a-lifetime transactions.

- **Oil and gas holdings**. Another trigger event in which clients find our services to be helpful is their need to manage significant oil and gas holdings. They may be receiving royalty income, or they may wish to liquidate or sell an operating interest. We can help them attain a large savings on their current income tax liability as well as estate tax savings.

Anyone who is experiencing one or more of those triggers could benefit from Stewardship Legacy Coaching. These events and situations, if structured wisely, can contribute to building a strong legacy. Our clients have saved significant sums, gaining the financial freedom to pursue meaningful activities and to transfer greater wealth to the next generations and to charitable causes. By modeling wise stewardship to their families, they also have opportunities to transfer wisdom to them. Through tax-wise planning, they have been good stewards of the money that God entrusted to them.

CHAPTER 2 QUESTIONS TO CONSIDER

1. How did you score on the Thriving Family Legacy Assessment? What are the opportunities for improvement?

2. Do you have wealth in some of the assets that create trigger events and do you have a plan for wisely stewarding the future sale, gift, or disposition of those assets?

3. How confident are you that your current plan is a Zero Estate Tax plan and that your heirs wouldn't pay any of IRD "gotcha" Tax?

4. Should you consider retaining a Stewardship Legacy Coach to help guide your family and business in building a strong and lasting family legacy and to create a plan to wisely steward your assets and trigger events?

SECTION TWO

FAMILY LEGACY

CHAPTER 3

LIVING UP TO THE FAMILY NAME

A good name is rather to be chosen than great riches.

—Proverbs 22:1 (KJV)

The couple owned a thriving, second-generation business. Mother and father were committed Christians, well-respected in their church and community, and striving to raise their large family—they had three adult children and four younger, adopted ones—with good values, virtues, and character. But something was wrong.

I had been meeting with the family members for a few months, helping them plan their family legacy. I soon became aware of conflict between one of their daughters and her father. She was in her mid-twenties, and the conflict seemed to be below the surface. It was not a topic of conversation within the family. I doubt anyone outside the family would even have known about it, but it clearly existed, and at times it seemed to border on animosity.

When coaching families, we work as close as necessary with all the generations involved. Here, I learned that the father had raised all the children with the expectation that they would be involved in the business. He was a kind and gentle man in many ways, but he had somewhat of a driver personality. He had driven all the children academically in school and also on the job. That approach had not worked for this daughter. She felt alienated. She did not want to be involved in the business, but she felt that her parents and other family members, as well as the community, expected it of her.

We often encourage families to help the children and grandchildren get a sense of their own identity and destiny. That includes their identity in the family and community, but also involves their unique personality, purpose, and passions. What has God created *them* to do? It may be quite different from what He created their parents to do. And it may not be at all what their parents want them to do.

In working with this family, I spent time with each of the parents and their children individually, hearing their hearts, finding out what made them tick. What were they passionate about? What did they see as their purpose? It was clear that the daughter and father loved and respected each other, but she felt squeezed into his mold. Over time, those feelings had festered into resentment and put a rift in the relationship.

The daughter finally explained that her real passion was horses. She was wired more for art and nature than for business. Her parents had thought that horses were just a hobby, but she told us that if she could do anything that she wanted, it would be working in an equestrian ministry to help disabled children. She told us about the therapeutic bond that develops between such children and horses. Her eyes lit up as she shared this with her parents and me. This was clearly her passion and purpose and why she was created. She saw this not just as a hobby, but as a potential vocation and ministry that would have an impact on other people's lives and on the world.

At a meeting with her parents alone, I explored this with them. They had seen their daughter come to life. She had not been this way during the several years that she had felt as if she were in the vice grip of their expectations for her. Now they wanted to support *her* dream instead of just trying to force her into the family business, which had been *their* dream.

For the first time, it became obvious to her father that he had been hard on his children. His intentions had been good. He wanted the best for them, and so he had pushed them. He had been a taskmaster. They knew it, and their mother knew it, but he had been unaware, and these feelings had gone unspoken. Now, he confronted the truth that he had been crushing his daughter's spirit.

"I can see it now," he said. "I've just been too demanding. I cared more about my vision for her that I did about her own vision." Dad started weeping. Mom started weeping. I started weeping.

He apologized to his daughter. He apologized to the rest of the family, as well, and committed to lightening up and supporting each child as a unique creation, with a unique purpose and passion. And when he did so, the daughter was able to see how she had been reacting inappropriately in her relationships with her father and family. She had developed a resistant, rebellious spirit. She, too, apologized.

That remarkable moment between father and daughter is an example of what we call intergenerational reconciliation. To move forward, families often will need to heal hurts from the past. To do so, they first must recognize them and then deal with them. That lays the foundation to build stronger and healthier family relationships.

Building a strong family legacy often will require family members to focus on the following deep relational issues:

- Reconcile their relationships (sometimes horizontally between spouses or between siblings and sometimes vertically through the generations)
- Define and promote family values and virtues
- Discuss what it means to be part of the family and live up to the family name
- Be guided by God's word
- Leave nothing left unsaid that they will wish they had said

RECONCILING RELATIONSHIPS

Such tensions flow as an undercurrent in many families and often span generations. The conflicts might be between parent and child or could be with the grandchildren or other relatives. The issues differ from family to family. Sometimes they involve addictions, or delinquency, or a rebellious spirit.

Many parents are struggling to find the right path, whether they are raising younger kids, teenagers, or dealing with their adult children. Numerous books and other resources are available for parents of school-age children, but relatively few resources offer direction on how to be effective parents to adult children. The relationship must change. It cannot be the same as it was when they were living at home and their parents were fully responsible for them and had a greater level of authority and control. Nonetheless, in learning to interact with their adult children, couples have one of their greatest opportunities to build a powerful legacy.

As the kids mature into adults (or, sometimes, fail to mature), parents often find it difficult to determine the appropriate role to play in their lives. If these young men and women are heading in what seems to be the wrong direction, what then? How do you speak to their lives when the relationship and the dynamic have changed? If you have made parenting mistakes along the way, how do you move past that for a healthy communication? You need to reconcile the relationship before intergenerational mentoring and discipleship can occur.

> In learning to interact with their adult children, couples have one of their greatest opportunities to build a powerful legacy.

The situations are as diverse as the individuals themselves. As we saw in chapter 1, children sometimes feel a sense of entitlement that stems from their affluence. Sometimes parents dictate their vocational vision for their children or require them to attend a certain college because the family has gone there for generations. If left unchecked, these attitudes have the potential to do a lot of damage.

Lack of trust, poor communication, or unhealthy family dynamics can destroy a lot of wealth, as well. People often believe that the biggest risk to successful wealth transfer or business succession is poor technical planning, and sometimes it is. But more often, family dysfunctions are what get in the way. The poor dynamics can led to family feuds in which nobody wins except the lawyers.

> The business of being a family is more important than the family business.

One third-generation business leader put it this way: "If our factory burned down, it would be tough, but we would get through it. However, if the family fell apart, we wouldn't get through it." He was saying that the business of being a family is more important than the family business. He recognized that the family legacy is an essential investment and worth spending time and money to invest in.

LIVING UP TO FAMILY VALUES

Historically, the family name has meant something. The surname often reflected the prevailing family vocation; members of the Smith family, for example, were silversmiths or blacksmiths. The Jewish people were known as the children of Abraham, Isaac, and Jacob. The family land holdings also were significant. In the biblical year of Jubilee, every half-century, the debt on land was to be forgiven. Such was the importance placed on the family.

In the biblical account of Ruth and Boaz, we see a powerful example of those themes of family, honor, and tradition. Boaz lived up to his family name and chose to marry and provide for Ruth, even though he was not the first family member directly in the line of responsibility. He became the "kinsman redeemer," honoring the family name.

Through the centuries, generation after generation, the family legacy was deemed to be of high value. Today, the significance of the family legacy seems to be getting lost. Many people do not feel that same responsibility to live up to the family name, and, very often, they do not. And yet we need to affirm that it is a worthy pursuit. We need to inspire the generations that follow us to live up to the family name, to be patriotic Americans, to live as citizens of heaven should, and to stand tall as ambassadors of the King of Kings.

We need to pass on the virtues, character, and values that determine our legacy. To do so, we must rise to the challenge of intergenerational mentoring and discipleship of our children and grandchildren. If you do not like the values that you see currently exhibited by them, what are you doing about it? Do you just sigh and say, "Well, I guess that's how young people are nowadays"? Or do you interact with them to communicate the values that you know will help them live a thriving, joy-filled life?

In helping people build a thriving family legacy, we seek to bring the generations together, working to heal any wounds and promote reconciliation, if necessary, so that families might pass on their wisdom as well as their wealth. Our goal is to help families instill their core values—their faith, wise stewardship, a heart for ministry, a passion of generosity—in the rising generations.

Wealth comes in many forms. You can think of wealth as the four Vs, consisting of vision, virtues, values, and valuables. These are all part of what you should be passing on. Your valuables are highly important but merely a part of your wealth. The money is not the end all. It is not the only form of capital that you can invest. Along with your financial capital, you have relational capital, intellectual capital, human capital, and spiritual capital.

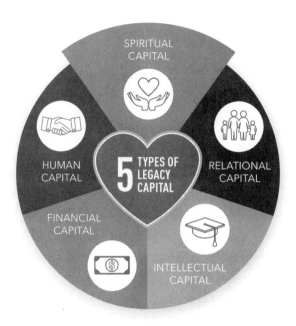

This is a broader vision of wealth transfer. It is more than the usual financial, legal, and tax considerations. As important as all of that is, it's not enough. You must also transfer your wealth of wisdom.

If you transfer only your wealth without wisdom, you can actually do your children and grandchildren more harm than good. They would be better off receiving only your wisdom without your wealth, because, in that way, you would provide them the means to earn their own wealth. The good news is that it isn't a zero-sum game. You can pass on both wealth and wisdom to your children, grandchildren, and future generations, a great way to build your family legacy to new heights.

GUIDED BY GOD'S WORD

In the Word of God, we find the keys to building such a legacy. There is a biblical model and principle for providing an inheritance for your children. "A good man leaves an inheritance to his children's children," we read in Proverbs 13:22 (NASB). In the words of Solomon, we are advised to think intergenerationally: not just think about our children, but also about our grandchildren.

In America today, most people leave all their wealth to their children. They often do not consider opportunities to invest in their grandchildren, or potentially, their own parents, or even the charities that are dear to their hearts. They just leave it all to their children. Their intentions are good, but often, the children get too much too easily. Often, the children haven't been properly prepared with the virtues, values, and wisdom needed to wisely manage all that wealth. Instead of it being the blessing the parents intended, it can become a curse. Instead of empowering and equipping, it can lead to an entitlement mentality and the lack of a work ethic. Although well intended, Mom and Dad may not be thinking holistically or biblically about what they are doing.

In the Old Testament, God indicated that a double portion of the inheritance should go to the eldest son. With that inheritance, however, came responsibility. The eldest son was expected to use that double portion to provide for his parents when they became aged and unable to care for themselves.

Today, wealth is transferred mostly via financial assets. Back in the day, it wasn't so. Before the industrial age, America was primarily an agricultural and trade/craft society. People owned farms. They had not only acreage but also livestock. Passing on an inheritance often meant that you were carving off sections of your land where your newly married children could build their own homes and work the land to earn a living. Or if you were a blacksmith, you trained and mentored your children and they took over the family business when you could no longer run it. In other words, you granted the inheritance, or at least part of it, before your death. You would do the giving while you were living.

That type of inheritance, and its biblical precedent, is the sort that requires work and effort on the part of the beneficiaries. It is not mere money, as is so often the case with inheritances today that require the receivers to do nothing but open their palms. When people are working to improve their situation, they tend to feel better about themselves. They feel they are productive members of society. They take satisfaction in looking back and knowing that they made it by the sweat of their brow. Those who make it by someone else's largesse may simply become slackers.

As with that double portion of inheritance to the eldest son, any inheritance should come with responsibility. "To whom much has been given, much will be required," we read in Luke 12:48 (AMP). Work is good. Sometimes people think that our need to work is a curse from Genesis, but God created us to cultivate (steward) the garden, to flourish, and thrive. Our labor became more difficult after the Fall, amid thorns and thistles, but that does not mean that work displeases God. He himself worked for six days and rested on the seventh, and He made us in His image.

The word of God truly needs to be central in building a family legacy, and that foundation of faith should be central to what you are passing on. Here is God's admonition to us about family legacies. In Psalm 71:18 (NIV): "Even when I am old and gray, do not forsake me, my God, till I declare your power to the next generation, your mighty acts to all who are to come."

Sometimes parents wonder why their children or grandchildren do not follow their faith, or drift away from it, or do not follow it passionately. If you are feeling that way, consider whether it could be because you have yet to truly share the great and wondrous works that God has done in your life. Share the story of your life's journey and your journey of faith and why your faith means so much to you.

LEAVE NOTHING LEFT UNSAID

One topic of conversation has risen to the surface as being the most compelling: Leave nothing left unsaid that you will wish you had said. Words such as "I love you" or "I'm sorry" or "I'm so proud of you"—these are among the sentiments that people carry in their hearts but that far too often never come to their lips.

In my own family, we individually came to see that truth a number of years ago around the time that my mother went home to be with the Lord. None of us had ever doubted our love for one another. It was a given, so much so that we didn't much talk about it. Her sudden passing moved our hearts to the understanding that we had not been as expressive in our love for one another as we should have been. This was our opportunity to do better. We started hugging more and saying, "I love you" more within our family. We didn't just want each other to know it; we knew we should say it.

Many people, particularly those from earlier generations, grew up in families that were not very expressive. They don't hug much. They don't offer words of affirmation and appreciation. They are not so quick to say, "I love you." This needs to change!

In my years of working with families, I often have seen people wait until they are on their deathbed to make things right with their children, or with their parents. Sometimes it is the younger generation that finally voices those healing words to their elders. Such moments of reconciliation are certainly cause to rejoice, yet one must wonder how much sweeter life might have been for both if they only had made their amends twenty years earlier. They might have shared more loving and joyous lives together. Also, sometimes people intend to have that conversation and share those words when they or their parent get on their proverbial death bed, but unfortunately, sometimes death comes quickly and suddenly—and we never get a chance to share them with our loved one. Instead of healing and reconciliation, the survivor is often left with regret over words unsaid.

You can say the words in person, or over the phone. You can write a letter, or record a video, but do it now, while you can.

To a son:

- I love you, son and I believe God has great plans in store for you.

- I'm sorry I missed so many of your ball games while you were growing up.

To a daughter:

- I am so proud that you are the person you have become.

- I'm sorry I missed so many of your recitals.

To your spouse:

- Your faithfulness has meant the world to me and to our family.

To your parents:

- Thank you for how you raised us, and provided for us, and invested in us.

To your grandparents:

- Thank you for standing firm on this family's values and for being *you*.

- Thank you for the godly wisdom you have shared with me and for the example of your life; you have inspired me!

- Thank you for the strong family legacy and values you have instilled in our family.

This is my challenge to you: Don't wait. As you build a strong family legacy, loving and candid communication is one of the most important skills of all. If you have something in your heart that needs to be said, say it right now. Leave nothing left unsaid that you will wish you had said!

BEYOND THE FAMILY

As you think about your legacy and the words you need to say, consider the important people in your life outside your immediate family. Is there anything you want to tell them? Do you have words of reconciliation, affirmation, gratitude, or encouragement to share?

Look back over the years and think of a teacher, a coach, a manager, or other mentor who made a difference in your life. A simple thank you means so much, and you could also show appreciation by becoming a mentor yourself to the younger men or women whom God has put in your sphere of influence.

I have been blessed to have a lot of good mentors, starting with my father, and including some godly pastors, good teachers and coaches, and great business and ministry people. If you have been likewise blessed, give those people a call or write them a letter sharing how their influence has helped shape your life.

My most influential teacher was Mike Simoneau. He taught history and social studies, ran the chess club, and coached soccer—and he had a phenomenal love for his students. At a pivotal point in my life, when I was a juvenile delinquent in junior high, he saw in me what few other people did, including me. He inspired me to become the best version of myself.

In my first job out of college, at a big corporation where I worked in accounting and finance, the department director called me into his office one day. I was only twenty-three but had visions of venturing out into a new career (which became my calling). My immediate manager and coworkers scoffed at the idea and told me I would fail and I should just stay there with them in the J-O-B. "Jeff, you are too young to fail," the director told me. "You will be successful at whatever you do. And even if it doesn't work out, you can always get a job at place like this." They were just the words that I needed to hear. He helped me to fly.

So did another corporate executive early in my financial services career, a former pastor named Bill Fortner. I was having serious doubts early in my new venture, and he could tell I was struggling. Bill asked me; "Jeff, has God ever failed anybody? "I thought quickly through the Old Testament and the New Testament and couldn't think of a single time that God had failed anybody. So I said,

"No, I don't think so, Bill." He went on to say, "Jeff, if God ever failed you, you would be the first person in all of human history that God failed, and Jeff, you're not that important to go down in history as the first person that God failed." We reconnected online recently, and I told him how grateful I was for those long-ago words. He had blessed me, and now my appreciation encouraged him, in return, as he heard how, thirty years earlier, he had given life-affirming counsel to a young man in need.

Think about such people who challenged you, inspired you, encouraged you, and mentored or discipled you. Have you ever said thank you? Write down their names and get in touch and also write down the names of people with whom you may need to reconcile. The time is now for healing.

You can visit our website at www.stewardshiplegacy.com/resources for some helpful resources on leaving nothing left unsaid.

CHAPTER 3 QUESTIONS TO CONSIDER

1. Have you created written vision, mission, and family values statements to help inspire and guide your children, grandchildren, and future generations? (If not, and you would like assistance, contact us!)

2. Who are the people who have influenced your life the most? What did you learn from each of them? What life lessons would you like to share with your children and grandchildren?

3. What could you do or say to let those key influencers in your life know how grateful you are for them? (I recommend scheduling a time on your calendar to think and pray this through and create a plan to tell each of them how much they mean to you. Go see them, write a letter, if you have to, give them a call, but leave nothing unsaid that you will wish you had said!

4. Are there others in your life to whom you need to say things such as "I love you," "I'm so proud of the person you've become," "I'm sorry … Will you forgive me?" Don't wait until you're on the proverbial death bed to share these things! Begin the process of reconciliation and healing now and make the rest of your time on earth count! Make some positive memories!

CHAPTER 4

SHIRTSLEEVES TO SHIRTSLEEVES

An inheritance gained hastily in the beginning
will not be blessed in the end.

—Proverbs 20:21 (ESV)

You may have heard the old saying, "shirtsleeves to shirtsleeves in three generations." It expresses a common but sad phenomenon: The first generation builds the wealth. The second generation tries to maintain it but drifts away from the founding values, and by the third generation, the wealth has been squandered. The saying is known around the world in varying forms. In China, it's "rice paddies to rice paddies in three generations." In old England, it was "clogs to clogs in three generations."

Let's take a look at that principle in the example of two famous families, the Vanderbilts and the Rothschilds. The first story is an example of what typically happens as wealth is passed down. The second is an example of what can happen when wealth is measured in more than money and when the patriarchs are intentional about transferring wisdom along with wealth; values as well as their valuables.

WEALTH TRANSFER
Shirtsleeves to shirtsleeves
in 3 generations

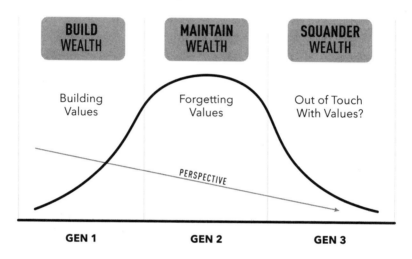

Cornelius Vanderbilt died in 1877 as the richest man in America, with an estate exceeding $105 million at the time. By the 1970s, there was not one millionaire among the dozens upon dozens of family descendants. The wealth had been transferred without responsibility or accountability—without wisdom. Instead of exhibiting virtue, values, and unity, the Vanderbilt family displayed jealousy, division, and strife. Instead of working hard, they flaunted their wealth with reckless spending, throwing lavish parties, proving that there is no amount of wealth too large that it can't be squandered. The pattern had been clear by the third generation, when Cornelius's grandson William K. Vanderbilt had this to say about the family's money: "It has left me with nothing to hope for, nothing definite to seek or strive for. Inherited wealth is a real handicap to happiness."

Mayer Amschel Rothschild (1744–1812), founder of a banking dynasty in Europe, taught his five sons the importance of wise stewardship and strong family values. The Rothschilds established a "family bank," meeting regularly to discuss how to grow the fortune and how to make wise decisions. His third son, Nathan Rothschild, became a financial envoy for the British government. "It requires a great deal of boldness and a great deal of caution to make a great fortune," Nathan Rothschild said, "and when you have got it, it requires ten times as much wit to keep it." Today, the Rothschild fortune is estimated to be worth trillions of dollars.

You can see what spells the difference between a legacy that endures for generations and one that dissipates to the point where the descendants can be left penniless. Building that strong legacy requires more than technical planning. It requires trust, communication, and preparing of your heirs.

A survey by Family Office Exchange, a peer network for ultra-wealthy families, asked affluent families what they considered their biggest risk to the transfer of their wealth. Forty-one percent pointed to estate and financial planning risks, investment risks, portfolio risks, management risks, timing risks, style risks, and business risks. Thirty-six percent pointed to risks involving the economy and financial markets, such as economic downturns, inflation, deflation, energy costs, and availability. Sixteen percent believed that their biggest challenges were political in nature, such as higher income and estate taxes, government intervention, and legal liability. Only 7 percent of those families felt that problems with family dynamics and relationships were the biggest threat, including poor communications, failure to pass on values, and family governance issues.

However, when we look closely at why wealth transfer fails, those are the issues that 90 percent of the time are at the root of it.[1]

However, when the survey looked back at the actual causes of failure in intergenerational wealth transfer, they found that 60 percent of the failure is due to a lack of communication and trust within the family. Thirty-seven percent of the failure is due to a lack of preparation of the heirs—the children and grandchildren—either in the area of family values or character virtues, or in terms of their ability to run the business or to manage the assets. Only 3 percent of the failure is due to failures in financial planning, taxes, and investments.

RISK PERCEPTION "What Do I Think Will Bite Me?"

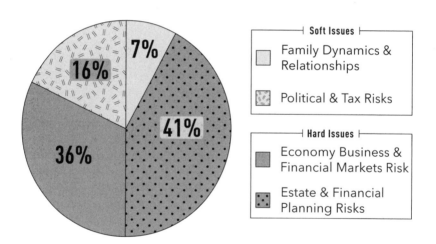

Soft Issues

☐ Family Dynamics & Relationships

▨ Political & Tax Risks

Hard Issues

■ Economy Business & Financial Markets Risk

⊡ Estate & Financial Planning Risks

---

1   Roy Williams and Vic Preisser, *Preparing Heirs: Five Steps to a Successful Transition of Family Wealth and Values* (Bandon: Robert Reed, 2010).

RISK PERCEPTION "What Bit Me?" Why Do 90% Fail?

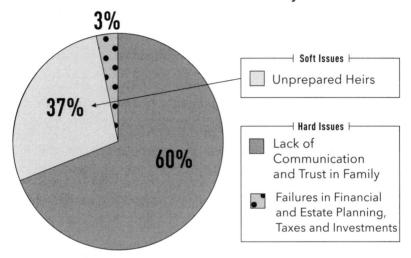

Soft Issues
☐ Unprepared Heirs

Hard Issues
▨ Lack of Communication and Trust in Family

▨ Failures in Financial and Estate Planning, Taxes and Investments

3%
37%
60%

Clearly, the perceptions and realities are diametrically opposed. People may think that family dynamics, trusted, relationships, and preparing heirs are a small part of the risks that they face in building a strong family legacy, whereas in truth those elements are by far the major part. Those figures dramatically illustrate that wisdom transfer must go hand-in-hand with wealth transfer. Children need to inherit not just money but also virtues (character), values, and wisdom. They need to inherit a strong work ethic. They need to be inspired by their purpose and passion. They need to have a sense of their identity and destiny, both as individuals and as a family.

In this chapter, we will establish that the successful passing of wealth to the next generations requires strong family dynamics and trusted relationships. To build an enduring family legacy, the wealth must be transferred in tandem with wisdom.

Because the biggest risk to the financial assets is family dysfunction, we will examine the importance of:

- The unity of spouses within a household
- The values that reside within a family
- The ability to cultivate a strong work ethic
- The task of preparing wise stewards

SPOUSAL UNITY

If both wealth and wisdom are to be passed on effectively, husband and wife must be of like mind when it comes to financial capital as well as relational, human, intellectual, and spiritual capital.

In my many years as an advisor and coach to families, I often have found that the husband prefers to come in alone, without his wife. Sometimes it has been because the wife is not interested in finances or planning, and he simply can't get her to come along. In other cases, the husband just wants to handle it all himself, out of a sense of control. Either way, it is not a healthy situation.

Several years ago, when I was on a business trip, I got a message from my staff suggesting that I pray for one of my clients who had been taken to the hospital. "He's not expected to come out this time," the message said. I prayed for the couple, but by the time I had returned home to Orlando, he had passed away. I said another prayer for the family, and the next day I called their house, expecting to talk to the widow. Instead, one of their sons answered the phone.

I had never met the son or any of the children, who lived in different states, but as I offered my condolences, the son told me this: "Jeff, you don't know what a blessing you've been to my mom and dad and to our family. When my dad went into the hospital this time, he knew he wasn't coming out. One of the things he told my mom was, 'If something happens, call Jeff. He knows the plan and where everything is. He'll take care of you.'"

Wow! My eyes welled up with tears when I heard that. That's what it's all about. It's so important that *both* husband and wife maintain a relationship with their advisors. When the day of sadness arrives, the surviving spouse should be able to set aside all worries so that he or she can grieve. In other situations, new clients will come in to see me after the spouse's funeral and they don't know where anything is. The finances are a scattered mess. The business blows up. They don't have that peace of mind.

I often have encouraged both husbands and wives to gain an understanding *together* of the workings of their financial lives, at least at a high level. That way, when something happens—because eventually it will, for all of us—the survivor will have the confidence that there is a plan and will know whom to call. While husband and wife both are alive, they also should build a relationship with the planner, and with the planning team, including an estate planning attorney, financial advisor, and a tax professional. It is important to have a team of advisors who can provide counsel in various areas. Often that team should be guided by a Family Legacy Coach who can help focus the team on the family's overall vision and values and their family legacy objectives.

I have strived to apply these principles personally. Our family recently underwent what some call a "lifeboat drill" and others call the "ultimate dress rehearsal." We gathered our whole team together at a resort in the Colorado mountains. These were good friends who would be helping Cathy with the transition if anything were to happen to me. They included our estate planning attorney, the trustees of our trust, the individual who would serve as Cathy's financial advisor, and also those who would be involved in our business succession.

We spent two days going over the what-if's. What if Jeff had gone Home to be with the Lord yesterday? We looked at a wide range of issues, including finances and estate, the business transition and succession, and the legal documents involved in each and every area. We laid out a plan so that Cathy would be familiar with it. She knows all the planners, and each member of the team knows the other members of the team and their respective roles.

Such thorough preparation expresses love and caring at a high level. Have you ever gathered all your advisors and closest friends and family at the same time to discuss your plans? Have you ever held your own ultimate dress rehearsal or lifeboat drill?

CULTIVATING A WORK ETHIC

I grew up in a middle-class family that shopped at Sears, as did many others in the 1960s and 1970s. Almost everything in our house came from Sears. We got the spring catalog, the fall catalog, the Christmas Wishbook catalog. Every appliance was a Kenmore. Every tool in the garage was a Craftsman. Some families shopped at JC Penney. We were Sears people.

My parents bought us Tough Skin jeans, a Sears brand with knee patches that must have been made of titanium. You couldn't wear those things out! When I was in my early teens, I decided I wanted Levi jeans instead. The Tough Skins were just not cool enough for me. And I wanted Converse All-Star or Nike sneakers instead of the Sears brand of sneakers.

"Well, Jeff, we pay for the Sears brand," my father told me. "If you want those fancy brands, we'll give you the money we would have paid, but you need to go out and earn the difference."

I know now what I didn't see then: my parents were teaching me the value of a dollar. They would provide for my needs, and for some of my wants, but to get some of my other wants, I had to earn and spend my own dollars. And in that way, my parents also were teaching me the value of work.

My mom and dad, children of the Great Depression, certainly wanted my brother and sister and me to have more than they did when they were growing up, and so they worked hard to make that happen. My father worked two jobs at times, sometimes three, just to provide well for us. At the same time, he studied at night to become an electrochemical engineer. He was determined to make something of himself and he wanted to be successful for his family. My mother also worked outside the home for a number of years.

They provided those resources out of love and caring—and they also withheld some of those resources out of love and caring. They understood the balance in a way that is lost on many people who feel their children should never have to struggle. They inspired me to work hard, to earn a living, to save for the things I wanted. My first jobs were mowing lawns, raking leaves, stacking wood, shoveling snow. I became a young entrepreneur, learning how to earn my customers' trust, to work hard and be reliable.

Along the way, I learned the concept of value creation. It's an important principle because it is the foundation of free enterprise, capitalism, and American exceptionalism. By creating value for others, entrepreneurs and businesses create value for themselves and their families. Through my labor of raking, mowing, and shoveling,

I created that value. I saved some of my money to be able to buy the things that I wanted, such as those Levis and Nikes.

I have often heard parents and grandparents complain about the lack of initiative in the younger generations. They feel dismayed at the attitude of entitlement in so many young people. My question to them is this: What are you doing about it? How are you inspiring and encouraging your children and grandchildren to learn the importance of hard work and the value of a dollar?

> How are you inspiring and encouraging your children and grandchildren to learn the importance of hard work and the value of a dollar?

Often we can help young people best by not making life too easy for them. One of my early jobs was at a full service gas station. I pumped gas, washed windshields, and changed oil and tires. That's less than pleasant work in midwinter. Those service bays, with all that cold steel, can feel like a deep freeze. I learned, frankly, that I hated that job. I determined that I would not be doing it for the rest of my life. That in itself was a valuable lesson. Such experiences can be quite motivating.

We can also combat the spirit of entitlement by encouraging young people to serve those who are less fortunate than themselves, whether by joining a group that feeds the homeless or volunteering at a rescue mission. Our nation and our global community unfortunately offer many such opportunities, and those experiences can help young people look beyond themselves to the needs of those in the world who are less well-off and appreciate their own blessings. If you already volunteer to help people in need, share the experience. Bring your children and grandchildren with you; make it a family time of serving and giving back! Let your children and grandchildren see the causes that break your heart and help them to discover what breaks their own hearts—and what breaks the heart of God!

Young people need to see, and experience, both the joys and struggles of life. I have heard so often in my career, from both parents and grandparents, this sentiment: "We want to make it easier for our kids than we had it growing up." Unfortunately, their efforts to make things easier could actually make things harder for their kids or grandkids in the long run.

If you are one who feels that the next generation should have it easy, consider whether your own struggles might have strengthened you. By providing too much, could you be denying the rising generations the opportunity to grow by overcoming obstacles and learn the benefits of hard work and initiative? Yes, you want to watch them thrive, but to avoid all hardship can be counterproductive to that end.

We see this in nature. When a caterpillar is breaking free of its cocoon, something good happens through its struggle and effort. It builds its strength, it develops its wings. It goes through the process of metamorphosis to become the butterfly it was meant to be. What happens if we, as humans, "help" the caterpillar by breaking open its cocoon in order to help it avoid the struggle and hard work to break itself out? We all know from biology that the caterpillar never develops its strength. It cannot fly and soon dies. It never becomes the beautiful butterfly it was created to be.

That principle holds true with our children and grandchildren. If we remove all hardship, all struggle, and all effort with the goal of making life easy for them, they will never develop into the "beautiful butterflies" they were created to be.

I'm fond of a quote often attributed to Robert Frost: "Americans are like a rich father who wishes he knew how to give his sons the hardships that made him rich."

Life presents many challenges. We learn to cope as we get through them. If our children and grandchildren do not learn how to overcome and achieve at a young age, they won't know how to deal with bigger obstacles—and opportunities—later in life, whether in adolescence or adulthood. God knows what it takes to create beautiful butterflies, and He knows what it takes to create beautiful people.

PREPARING WISE STEWARDS

One of the responsibilities of parents or grandparents is to prepare our children and grandchildren to be wise stewards who will not just survive but thrive!

One of the questions many families struggle with is: Should we give to all of our children equally or should we give to them based on their needs or how well they will likely manage it? I like the way my friend Ron Blue, founding director of Kingdom Advisors, puts it in his book *Splitting Heirs*. Ron says, "We should love our children equally but treat them uniquely."

> We should love our children equally but treat them uniquely.

Each child will have a different set of circumstances. For example, special-needs children may lack the capacity to handle a large financial inheritance but may need care or services throughout their lifetime. Other children may struggle with personal problems—an addiction, for example, or a gambling problem—that they will need to overcome before gaining significant access to the family wealth. Others may have invested significant "sweat equity" in learning and working in the family business. In other words, the children will have greater or lesser needs, and the wealth transfer can be adjusted accordingly. Our love, however, should be given equally to all our children and grandchildren. Though we are meeting unique situations, we still love them equally.

In Ecclesiastes 7:11-12 (NIV), we read these words: "Wisdom, like an inheritance, is a good thing and benefits those who see the sun. Wisdom is a shelter as money is a shelter, but the advantage of knowledge is this: Wisdom preserves those who have it." The references to wisdom abound in the Bible—in Ecclesiastes, in Proverbs, and in numerous other places.

Our society seems to be losing its appreciation of wisdom. We live in the information age, where everything is about knowledge. The best definition of wisdom I have ever heard is that "wisdom is the correct application of knowledge." Knowledge applied incorrectly can render us fools.

If you want to help your family to become wise and responsible stewards and people of integrity, initiative and hard work, you should be asking what this child (or grandchild) needs to know, how this child needs to develop, which virtues this child should develop, and how that wisdom can best be imparted. That requires far more than some brain dump of knowledge that we think we should impose. Education is valuable, indeed, but when bestowed with wisdom and experience and guided by virtues and values, the combination is priceless.

What life lessons and guiding principles have you learned that

What life lessons and guiding principles have you learned that should be taught to your children and grandchildren?

should be taught to your children and grandchildren? What are the stories of your life and journey that the next generation needs to hear? Is there wisdom that you learned from your parents or grandparents, teachers, coaches, and mentors that would be valuable for your kids and grandkids to learn? Could they also learn from your mistakes as well as your successes?

As you prepare your family for the transfer of your financial assets, be sure to also share what is in your head and your heart. Transferring wisdom along with wealth is the best defense against the shirtsleeves-to-shirtsleeves syndrome. It's the best way to safeguard the family wealth as you build a legacy that will endure for many generations.

CHAPTER 4 QUESTIONS TO CONSIDER

1. Do you have a well-thought-out, intentional plan to avoid the shirtsleeves-to-shirtsleeves 90 percent failure of inherited wealth statistic in your children and grandchildren? If not, should you create such a plan?

2. How well prepared are your children and grandchildren to receive and wisely steward inherited wealth? What could you do to help them be better prepared in the areas of work ethic, understanding the value of a dollar, managing finances well, or in running a business?

3. Given the importance of transferring wisdom along with wealth, what are the key life lessons and nuggets of wisdom you've learned (either through wise mentors or through the school of hard knocks) that would benefit your children, grandchildren, and future generations? (Write them down and share them!)

4. In the past, have you and your spouse made the (well-meaning) mistake of trying to make life too easy for your children or grandchildren? If so, how can you reverse that trend? (If you need a guide to assist you, please contact us! We're here to help families like yours!)

SECTION THREE
FINANCIAL LEGACY

CHAPTER 5

HOW MUCH IS ENOUGH?

I have seen a grievous evil under the sun: wealth hoarded to the
harm of its owners, or wealth lost through some misfortune, so that
when they have children, there is nothing left for them to inherit.

—Ecclesiastes 5:13–14 (NIV)

The husband and wife were miles apart on how to divide the family wealth, to the point where the conflict was beginning to divide them as a couple. Thanks to a third-generation business—the husband was the grandson of the founder—the family was financially blessed, with a net worth in excess of $100 million.

The big question was how much money would be appropriate to leave to the children. In working with the couple, we noted right away the husband's deep concern that too much could harm their children. He felt that $1 million or $2 million for each child would be reasonable. His wife, however, felt that what would be best for the children would be to give them enough so that it would produce $1 million per year in income to the kids so they could maintain the lifestyle the parents had provided for them—perhaps $20 million for each child. Through several extended meetings and conversations, we helped them to think and pray this through. Eventually, they found a place of agreement at about $5 million for each child.

The discussions helped the couple to come together in unity, with much less tension in their relationship, and to gain clarity about a higher purpose for the remainder of their wealth. Having defined and quantified an appropriate inheritance, they were able to move forward to be even more generous to their church and to the charities and ministries they supported. The amount differs from family to family, but it's important to determine an appropriate inheritance.

In this chapter, we will look at the biblical guidance and practical applications for families in deciding how much to spend on their own needs and wants, how much to leave as an inheritance, and how much to invest in the Kingdom of God. We will consider:

- How to strike the right balance with an inheritance: large enough to be a blessing, not so large as to become a curse

- How to set a financial finish line where you know your personal life goals and have enough resources to meet them

- God's ownership of all we have, and our responsibility to be good stewards

- Give generously to leave a legacy that can have an eternal impact

STRIKING A BALANCE

Though the Bible says that "a good man leaves an inheritance to his children's children," many couples struggle with how much is enough and what is an appropriate inheritance. One of the questions I often ask clients to consider is: "Do you think it is possible to give too much wealth to your children and grandchildren so that it could become a curse instead of a blessing and has the potential to harm them rather than help them?"

I have asked scores if not hundreds of families that question, and most tell me that they have never thought about inheritance that way. They almost always agree that it is possible to give their heirs too much, but they have never been asked that question before or asked it of themselves.

This is how Warren Buffett, chairman of Berkshire Hathaway and one of the world's wealthiest men, sees it: "I want to give my kids enough so that they would feel they could do anything they want, but not so much that they would feel like doing nothing."

The traditional paradigm for estate planning in America amounts to this: when you die, no matter how much you have, the IRS will get half of your assets and your children will get the other half. That presumption stops people from thinking beyond the next generation. Whatever the government doesn't take will go to the kids.

Wouldn't it be better to think about what would be an appropriate inheritance so that it would be a blessing and not a curse? Wouldn't it be better to think about inheritance in a multi-generational way (children and grandchildren) and even from an eternal perspective of giving to the causes and ministries that will impact our community and the world around us for good and for eternity?

Many middle-income families might feel that they would not be leaving enough to their children to do them harm, and that could well be so. Affluent families, however, need to think long and hard about that potential that Buffett so aptly describes. We don't want to rob our children or grandchildren of the many benefits of hard work, initiative, learning to spend, save, invest and—oh yeah—give generously to others.

I recently worked with a couple whose net worth was about $20 million and who were deeply concerned about the effect of an inheritance on their children. He had a son from a previous marriage who was in his twenties, and she had a twelve-year-old from a previous marriage.

"If you were to drop several million dollars into the hands of your son today," I asked the husband, "would that be a good thing or a bad thing?"

"That would be terrible," he said without hesitation. "I know what my son would do with that money. He would buy a new pickup truck and ATV and some other toys and have the time of his life for a few years. He probably would quit his job and just play for a while. It wouldn't be enough for him to live on forever, and it would probably end up doing him more harm than good."

The couple then considered how an inheritance might affect the younger child. The money would have to be kept in trust until he reached the age of maturity, but by then, if it were properly invested, he would have a huge amount of money—probably not a good thing for him. It could bring temptations and pressures and even be a magnet for the wrong kind of friends or girlfriends. They felt that, in their case, the result could be a train wreck.

Over the next few meetings, I walked them through a process that we call "quantifying how much is enough." We helped them to think through, discuss, and pray about what would be an appropriate inheritance for each of their sons. They arrived at a number that they felt would be a blessing to each of them but not so much that it would likely ruin them.

I had another business owner recently tell me "If my parents had given me a million dollars I would have been even more arrogant than I was!" Over the years, he has learned a lot of valuable lessons: the value of hard work, how to build and lead a business, how to spend wisely and give generously. In the process he has been humbled and instead of being prideful and self-centered, he now is a loving husband and dad and a mentor to younger business guys. I'm so glad his parents didn't ruin him!

You won't find many estate planning attorneys, financial advisors, or tax experts walking people through a process like that. Again: the usual presumption is that the children will get whatever the IRS leaves, whether that is an appropriate amount or not. Few people pause to consider, "How much is enough?" They generally don't think about the balance between how much would be a blessing for a good start in life versus how much might create a slacker or how too much wealth (too easily obtained) can lead to "affluenza."

AT THE FINANCIAL FINISH LINE

Somebody once asked John D. Rockefeller, the founder of Standard Oil, "How much is enough?" His answer: "Just a little bit more." After he died, someone asked his accountant how much John Rockefeller had left behind. The accountant wisely replied: "All of it." That will be true for all of us!

We live in a prosperous society, but one that often focuses on consumption. The desire for more, more and still more can keep people from ever reaching a place of contentment. In Proverbs 21:17 (NIV), we read: "Whoever loves pleasure will become poor; whoever loves wine and olive oil will never be rich." The Bible teaches that we will never feel we have enough of things that we idolize. We have all heard of people who seem to have attained the dream but feel an emptiness inside. They have the proverbial "Hole in their Soul." They lack contentment.

Overspending won't bring contentment, nor will stockpiling without purpose. Contentment requires clarity. It comes from knowing when the accumulation race is over and that enough is enough. Having accumulated wealth, it's time to define why it matters and who should benefit from it. Sooner or later, we each move from accumulating assets to distributing them. (All of us will do this eventually, voluntarily or involuntarily, planned or unplanned; but we will end up distributing all that we have accumulated during our lifetime or at its end. That brings us to the topic of setting a "financial finish line."

> Having accumulated wealth, it's time to define why it matters and who should benefit from it.

Family leaders need to decide where the finish line will be. Husband and wife should set a financial goal which will be the point where they will have accumulated sufficient resources to support their lifestyle and to provide for others in whatever way they feel called. They can't just guess (or shouldn't). They need to go about this process carefully and prayerfully with thoughtful analysis and thinking through the myriad of issues. Most need a guide to help them through this process. Most need a Family Legacy Coach to guide them and ask the right questions.

As couples consider where to set their financial finish line, here are just a few of the questions that they need to consider:

- How much is enough for us? What do we need to live the lifestyle that we believe God wants us to live for the balance of our lives? How much do we need annually for that? How much do we need to set aside in investments or assets so that we have prudently prepared for the balance of our lives?

- How much is enough for our children and grandchildren? How do we make sure that we leave an appropriate inheritance that is a blessing and not a curse, so that it helps them but doesn't hinder or harm them? Equally important, how do we prepare them to wisely steward it so the wealth doesn't ruin them and so they don't squander the wealth?

Christians may recognize that they should be doing more to help others or invest in the Kingdom, but they're not sure how or where to set their own financial finish lines. Until they can answer that first question—How much is enough for us?—it's hard to know how much will be enough for the kids and how much can be given to the charitable causes they care deeply about.

When that question goes unanswered, it can affect peace of mind and generosity. Let me ask you a question: Do you think that if either spouse is concerned about running out of money someday, they will err on the side of over-generosity or under-generosity? In almost every case, they will err on the side of under-generosity. Even families worth hundreds of millions of dollars sometimes harbor a concern that they may run out of money. Having a sense of true financial freedom (and contentment) is one of the huge benefits of quantifying how much is enough and setting a financial finish line!

In my experience, one of the spouses tends to feel more confident than the other about their financial future. Often, that person has been the primary earner and risk taker and tends to have an abundance mentality, believing that more will come and there will always be enough. The other spouse often is frugal (but sometimes a spender instead) and sometimes doesn't even know the extent of the couple's wealth. As a result, that spouse cannot see how the future will look, especially if the other spouse wasn't around or if the business or source of income was sold, and therefore that spouse is more prone to worry—or at least to wonder and often they don't have a deep sense of financial freedom.

> Having a sense of true financial freedom (and contentment) is one of the huge benefits of quantifying how much is enough and setting a financial finish line!

We help people gain the clarity they need without becoming formulaic or prescriptive. First, we help them examine their levels of spending, for both fixed and discretionary expenses. We help them determine their needs and how much those cost. And then we look at the areas of flexibility where spending and giving could be dialed up or down. We consider, as well, how much they spend on the pleasures of life. God is not against our enjoying what He has blessed us with. We must balance those pleasures, though, with the needs of the world around us.

After analyzing those areas of spending, we do a cash flow analysis where we look at rates of return, taxes and inflation, and the what-if's that could arise, such as medical and long-term care costs.

All of these measures are in the context of clearly established goals. What do our clients wish to achieve financially? How much do they wish to give? What do they want to do, personally or as a family? We analyze the numbers and help them to come up the goals that are appropriate for them.

We are not the lifestyle police. We help people to discover for themselves the numbers they need to reach their goals. Once they attain that clarity, they can feel confident in their own financial future—and decide on an appropriate inheritance for the children and grandchildren. We like to talk about the five Cs: confusion leads to conflict while clarity leads to increased confidence and contentment.

GOD'S OWNERSHIP, OUR STEWARDSHIP

In creating a financial legacy, we believe that the first and most foundational principle is that God is the owner of it all, and we are his stewards. That truth is expressed with beautiful clarity in 1 Chronicles 29:11–12 (TLB):

> Everything in the heavens and earth is yours, O Lord, and this is your Kingdom. We adore you as being in control of everything. Riches and honor come from you alone, and you are the Ruler of all mankind; your hand controls power and might and it is at your discretion that men are made great and given strength.

Psalms 24:1 (NIV) says simply, "The earth is the Lord's, and everything in it." Or in the words to an old hymn: "He owns the cattle on a thousand hills, the wealth in every mine."

Whatever we have, our Creator has given to us. He gives us each new breath and each new day is a gift from Him. He gives us our gifts, strengths, and talents, and the opportunities to use them. Yes, we may have worked hard to develop those talents and to expand our knowledge, but our ability to learn is also a gift from God.

Many people harbor the false notion of the self-made man or woman. In reality, there is no such thing. In fact, if you ask most wealthy people how they got that way, even non-Christians will say such things as: "We were fortunate," or "We were in the right place at the right time." I would say, "We are blessed!" We are indeed a very rich and very blessed people in this nation. Even our poor seem rich by the standards in so many places around the world, where poor people starve and lack clean water. Those blessings should lead us to a spirit of thanksgiving and an "attitude of gratitude." We have a responsibility to wisely steward and manage what we have been given. Question: Are you and your spouse modeling an attitude of gratitude to your children, grandchildren, and others around you?

The delusion of "family money" arises from people's belief that they are self-made. They believe that *they* created the wealth and it belongs to them, and that therefore they should keep it all in the family from generation to generation, regardless of the consequences. When we come to understand that it is God's money, and that He has allowed us to be His stewards, our perspective on the purpose of money changes. As Deuteronomy 8:18 (NIV) tells us: "Remember the Lord your God, for it is He who gives you the ability to produce wealth."

As my friend and mentor Howard Dayton says, "There is man's part, and there is God's part."

For example, the farmer's job is to till the soil, plant the seed, and pull the weeds. But, if God never sends the sunshine or provides the rain, nothing will grow. None of us could have, or do, or be anything without our Creator's gifts and blessings. God lets us enjoy the fruit of the trees—but they are *His* trees!

It only makes sense, then, as we consider the concepts of inheritance and family legacy, that we should be asking the Owner what He wants us to do with the resources that He has entrusted to us. As Ron Blue of Kingdom Advisors suggests, all individuals should be asking themselves these questions:

- Who is the owner of the wealth?

- How much is enough?

- Who is the next steward, and is he or she prepared?

These are questions that we help people answer through our Stewardship Legacy Coaching process.

INVESTING IN ETERNITY

In his book *The Treasure Principle*, Randy Alcorn points to Matthew 6:19–21 (NIV):

Do not store up for yourselves treasures on earth, where moths and vermin destroy, and where thieves break in and steal. But store up for yourselves treasures in heaven, where moths and vermin do not destroy, and where thieves do not break in and steal. For where your treasure is, there your heart will be also ...

No matter how much we accumulate in life, we will leave it all behind one day. The money, the houses, the cars, the business are here but for a season. When we invest in God's Kingdom, however, we are investing in eternity.

Once we understand the relationship of God's ownership and our stewardship, we can move forward responsibly to create a financial legacy. In 1 Timothy 6:17–19 (NIV), we find some great principles on responsible stewardship and use of wealth:

> Command those who are rich in this present world not to be arrogant nor to put their hope in wealth, which is so uncertain, but to put their hope in God who richly provides us with everything for our enjoyment. Command them to do good, to be rich in good deeds, and to be generous and willing to share. In this way, they will lay up treasure for themselves as a firm foundation for the coming age, so that they may take hold of the life that is truly life.

Note that this passage is written in the imperative voice. It is not a suggestion. It is a command "to those who are rich in this present world." I would say that describes almost all of us here in America. The passage also tells us not to arrogantly put our hope in wealth, but rather, in the certainty of God, who wants us to enjoy what He abundantly provides. In fact, He commands us to enjoy it. This is not some prescription for poverty. He wants us to live like children of the King, which is what we are as Christians.

The passage is clear, however, that we are *not to* just spend on ourselves. We are to be generous with our resources and our time. We are to think about those around us and put those resources to good use: to be "rich in good deeds."

The Bible speaks of three types of love: eros, phileo, and agape. Eros is the fleshly love between a man and a woman. Phileo is the love of mankind, or brotherly love, from which the city of Philadelphia gets its name. It is the love that wells up in the heart because of the blessings we have received, and it inspires us to give back to our community, mankind, and the world around us. But the highest form of love in the Greek language is agape, most often translated as *charity* in the King James version of the Bible. This is the kind of love that emanates from the heart of God, and it encompasses both caring for our fellow man and loving our Creator. It leads us to give sacrificially, out of hearts of compassion for humanity and God's Kingdom, out of hearts of gratitude to Him for His inexpressible love for us and His work of redemption in us. It inspires us to give out of hearts of gratitude because we love others but also because we love Him. That ought to be our motivation for giving generously, not merely some sense of legalistic duty.

The words *philanthropy* and *charity* often are used interchangeably in our culture, but each clearly derives from a different biblical expression of love. Philanthropy is the spirit of doing what is best for mankind and giving back. When you give out of charity, or agape love, the heart of God is moving you. I believe that the combination of philanthropy and charity is what leads to extravagant generosity.

By contrast, "biblical stewardship" involves managing God's resources in a way that will please the Owner. It involves not just how we give, but also how we spend, save, and invest. God wants us to be a good steward of 100 percent of what He entrusts to us for His purposes. That means more than just the 10 percent tithe. The late Larry Burkett, founder of Christian Financial Concepts which later became Crown Financial Ministries, explained that "God is just as concerned with how we spend and invest the other 90 percent as He is with how we give the first 10 percent!"

Biblical stewardship also expresses a heart of generosity. In that spirit, the question of how much is enough for ourselves and for our heirs also informs the question of how much can or should we give to bless others less fortunate than ourselves or to invest in God's Kingdom. Generosity springs from the heart of God, who gave His own Son because He so loved the world. His is the ultimate expression of generosity and the heavenly example of investing in that which is eternally significant! As we weigh how much is enough for our earthly needs and those of our children and grandchildren, we must remember the example of He who offered the ultimate sacrifice for us! John 3:16 (NIV) is probably the best-known verse in the Bible, even among non-Christians: "For God so loved the world that He gave …"!

CHAPTER 5 QUESTIONS TO CONSIDER

1. Have you set a financial finish line for yourselves so that you can get out of the rat race of mindless accumulation and consumption and experience contentment and true financial freedom?

2. Do you believe it's possible to give your children or grandchildren "too much" wealth so that instead of it being a blessing, it risks becoming a curse; instead of helping them, it could end up harming them? What can you do to quantify an "appropriate inheritance" so that it would empower your heirs but not create enablement or an attitude of entitlement?

3. When you consider God's ownership and our stewardship, how could you use giving and generosity as a way to break the bondage that money can have in our lives (and that of our heirs) and as a way of investing in something that will truly will provide an eternal legacy (God's Kingdom)? Remember that where your treasure is, there will also be your heart!

Most couples need help navigating these complex questions and coming to a place of clarity, confidence, and unity around them. They need a Family Legacy Coach to guide them, asking the right questions, presenting creative ideas and solutions. If you need a guide, contact us, we're here to help!

CHAPTER 6

DEATH TO TAXES

My people are destroyed for lack of knowledge ...

—Hosea 4:6 (KJV)

"In this world nothing can be said to be certain, except death and taxes," founding father Benjamin Franklin wrote, observing that the nation's new constitution might seem permanent, but who really knew? I appreciate his humor, and I agree with much of what Franklin had to say, but I must take exception with that particular observation. For one thing, I know that death is not inevitable for the Christian who has secured the promise of eternal life. And taxation—certainly federal estate taxes and capital gains taxes—can be optional to a great degree.

From Judge Learned Hand: "In America there are two tax systems; one for the informed and one for the uninformed. Both systems are legal. Anyone may arrange his affairs so that his taxes shall be as low as possible; he is not bound to choose that pattern which best pays the treasury. There is not even a patriotic duty to increase one's taxes. Over and over again the Courts have said that there is nothing sinister in so arranging affairs as to keep taxes as low as possible. Everyone does it, rich and poor alike and all do right, for nobody owes any public duty to pay more than the law demands."

Among the financially blessed families with which I have worked, I have seen common themes. The numbers change, the faces change, the personalities and the details change, but some things tend to be the same. Let me tell you about one such family.

The family had a very large estate, north of $100 million, which presented the dilemma of a huge amount in estate taxes. The wealth derived from a third-generation business founded decades ago by the current owner's grandfather. The business is one of the largest employers in the community, and the family is known to be generous givers to various charities.

When the family members came in to see us, their primary concern was about the potential impact that amount of wealth could have on the children. They were intrigued by the wisdom transfer and heir preparation parts of our process. From a wealth transfer perspective, they thought they already had a good plan. They had several attorneys, including a trusted business attorney. They had CPAs for both personal and business matters. They had money invested at several banks and other financial institutions, and they figured that was providing them with diversification.

Though they believed that they were on solid ground from a planning perspective, we discovered upon analyzing their situation that under the existing scenario, the federal estate and IRD tax would have been almost $38 million. Even very wealthy families and businesses generally do not keep $38 million in liquid assets. Their money is usually tied up in businesses, real estate, or other illiquid investments. As we saw in chapter 2, many of the people who become our clients are facing one or more of several significant trigger events. How they deal with those events can dramatically influence how much they or their heirs will owe in taxes.

This family realized, much to their shock, that they were at risk of a forced sale of the family business. The thriving enterprise upon which they had prospered for three generations would not have made it to the fourth generation. The estate taxes, due upon death, would have been overwhelming. In other words, they would have "killed" the "goose that lays the golden eggs." Instead, we showed them legal, financial, tax, and charitable strategies to eliminate the estate tax and secure their business legacy. In doing so, we helped them save all those local jobs that so many families depended upon, and they maintained and enhanced their ability to continue supporting so many worthy causes. They not only kept the "goose" alive but got it to lay more of those precious eggs. What's really ironic is that the government helped them pay for this advanced planning through tax savings!

Such a strategy requires wise planning. So that there is no misunderstanding, let me emphasize that I am not against paying taxes. I pay my fair share of taxes. In fact, I pay more than most people do. Jesus spoke about taxation in Mark 12:17 (ESV): "Render to Caesar the things that are Caesar's, and to God the things that are God's." I believe that we should pay every penny in taxes that we legitimately owe.

Nonetheless, the tax code provides a variety of means by which people can pay less in taxes if they abide by certain rules and requirements. Some of the wealthiest families in America have paid relatively little in estate taxes. The wealth of the Rothschilds, Kennedys, Rockefellers, and others has endured generation after generation. Why? Because their attorneys know the rules, and they follow them. The average person, however, and even the average wealthy person, often does not know all the rules. It reminds me of Hosea 4:6 (KJV): "My people are destroyed for lack of knowledge ..."

> **Inefficient tax management probably won't destroy you, but you could be throwing away huge opportunities.**

Inefficient tax management probably won't destroy you, but you could be throwing away huge opportunities. You could be taking advantage of a variety of techniques to save significant money in your current income taxes and in capital gains and estate taxes. Think of what you save as "found money." What you would otherwise have sent to the IRS in taxes or spent on probate fees, you instead can redirect to the causes you care deeply about.

The following three key principles can greatly impact resources you have available to help others or prepare for your future:

- The details of zero estate tax planning

- How to protect your assets for your heirs

- How to begin your estate planning, God's way

Are we just building "bigger barns" or building God's Kingdom?

ZERO ESTATE TAX PLANNING

As I pointed out in chapter 5, estate planning in America typically presumes that the IRS will get about half and the children will, by default, get the rest. The planning begins and ends there in over 90 percent of estate plans. We believe there is a better way.

In most cases, the concept of Zero Estate Tax Planning legally allows people to opt out of paying estate taxes. In that way, the remainder potentially could all go to the children—but of course that need not be the case. The big question is this: Even if it all could go to the children, would that be wise? Would that amount of wealth be helpful or potentially harmful to your children or grandchildren?

Sometimes it is. For example, we have clients in Texas who wanted the entire value of their $80 million estate and all their businesses to go to their children, who were running the businesses well. Their father had mentored them. Mom and Dad felt that they would be good stewards of those resources. In their case, we structured their plan so that 100 percent of the value of the estate would go to the children. We zeroed out the estate taxes so that they could keep all the wealth in the family, and, most importantly to them, keep the businesses in the family. To do this we utilized a combination of legal, tax, financial, and charitable strategies that allowed them to create a Zero Estate Tax plan while redirecting significant sums to their favorite ministries. It was what we call a win-win-win. They won with current tax savings, their children won by eliminating the tax and keeping the family business in the family, and God's Kingdom won as well. The only "loser"? Their least favorite "uncle": Uncle Sam, the IRS.

Very often, however, that is not the wise choice, as we saw in the last chapter. Too much inherited wealth can be a curse rather than a blessing. Still, let us not forget that "a good man leaves an inheritance to his children's children." Your planning might best serve your family if you make sure that *some* of the money goes to the grandchildren (usually in a protective trust or generation-skipping trust). Those funds could be designated for their education or other appropriate purposes such as a down payment on a home, seed money for starting a business, and so on.

> We show people a better way: how they can use Zero Estate Tax Planning to eliminate the tax and convert their "social capital," or taxes, into Kingdom Capital to do God's work.

Either way, however, you can get the IRS share down to nothing, eliminating the estate tax (and IRD tax). Some professional advisors merely aim to reduce the tax through discount valuation or compression techniques. The approach of many financial advisors (and life insurance agents) is simply to sell you a big life insurance policy to pay the tax with so-called discounted dollars. We show people a better way: how they can use Zero Estate Tax Planning to eliminate the tax and convert their "social capital," or taxes, into Kingdom Capital to do God's work.

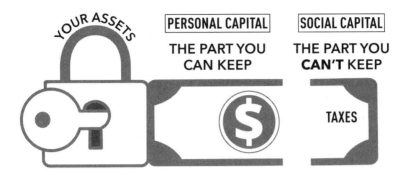

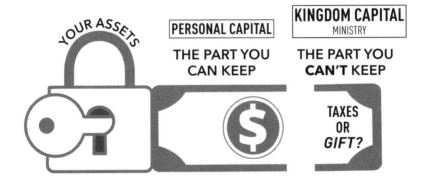

ASSET PROTECTION FOR YOUR HEIRS

In today's litigious society, we believe that it's wise, when leaving wealth to your children or grandchildren, to do so in a structure that will protect it for them. You can protect the inheritance from creditors and predators and from frivolous lawsuits. You can prevent the money from being lost in a divorce settlement. I have heard people hesitate to leave money to a daughter for fear that, God forbid, she would get a divorce, and the money would end up in the hands of the "scoundrel" who had been their son-in-law.

Such a structure also can protect the money not only *for* the children and grandchildren but also, if necessary, *from* them. Some young people clearly have a propensity to spend wildly. As did the prodigal son, they are likely to squander their inheritance unless appropriate controls and boundaries are built around it. You will want to be particularly cautious if you know that one or more of your heirs is a poor money manager who is inclined to rack up debts and who does not make prudent decisions related to boyfriends or girlfriends, or husbands or wives.

You also may want to put such protections in place if the heir is any kind of an addict. One of our clients, an elderly widow, struggled with the question of how to leave an appropriate inheritance to her adult son, a talented artist but a troubled man who had struggled for many years with substance abuse and emotional problems. For periods of time, he had lived in his car, homeless, by choice. She wanted to leave money to her church and to various ministries, but she also wanted to do what was right by her son.

"I believe what you're saying," I told her, "is you want to protect the money *for* him, but you also want to protect the money *from* him." She agreed. We showed her how she could set up a charitable remainder trust, to be funded upon her passing, from which her son could have a limited monthly income stream to meet basic needs but could never touch the principal. Upon his death, the money would go to charity, and in the meantime it would be protected from creditors and lawsuits. She felt the concept was custom made for her situation. She wanted to provide "a roof over his head and food in his belly," but little more. She wanted him to have to work for his wants, but she wanted to provide for his basic needs.

There would be some requirements. He would have to submit to random drug and alcohol testing. He would have to prove to the trustee that he was being a productive member of society and not falling back into addiction. If he did so, the trust would distribute the income. If he did not, the tap would be turned off. You might think of that as a faucet trust: one that flows only for appropriate and responsible behavior. The flow ceases when it would do more harm than good. (This "faucet" technique can also be done with some properly designed non-charitable trusts).

Asset Protection Trust: Protect the assets *for* your heirs ... and *from* your heirs.

Every client's situation is different, and the laws on trusts vary from state to state. It's important to work with somebody who knows your family dynamics and your situation, who understands your heart and what you want to accomplish for your children and grandchildren and for the charities that you wish to support.

You will need a Family Legacy Coach who can coordinate and convene your professional advisory team—the lawyers, accountants, and others—so that all are working together toward your purposes— and especially toward the purposes of your Creator, the Owner of it all. How does He wish you to handle the resources that He has entrusted to you? Are you being a good steward, are you clear on how much is enough, and have you chosen and prepared the next stewards? It's almost impossible to navigate yourself and your own family through what can be a potential minefield of mistakes that can ruin your family. People need a guide who is experienced in combining effective Wealth Transfer with intentional Wisdom Transfer; a guide who will ask you the right questions and present creative ideas and solutions. If you need a guide, contact us—we're here to help!

ESTATE PLANNING GOD'S WAY

When it comes to estate planning, you have some choices about how your wealth will be redistributed when you have left this earth. You can do it Uncle Sam's way, which is a forced redistribution via taxation to take care of the government's priorities, or you can do it God's way so that you can support the priorities of He who really owns the wealth.

Either way, you will be a philanthropist. You will be handing over a large sum for others to use. You can do so either by paying estate and IRD taxes and ceding to the politicians the decisions on where it will go, or else you can decide for yourself where it will go; giving it to causes and organizations that you feel deeply about. In other words, you can be an involuntary philanthropist or a voluntary steward.

Traditional, secular estate planning often is based on incorrect assumptions. One is that "it's all about me and my family." The truth is that *it is not about you,* as Rick Warren points out in the first sentence of the first chapter of *The Purpose Driven Life.* Another false premise is that you own your wealth. We know that God is really the ultimate Owner. We are His stewards. And a third incorrect assumption is this: "I built my wealth and it's my family's money." Take a look again at Deuteronomy 8:18 (NIV) for clarity on that matter: "But remember the Lord your God, for it is He who gives you the ability to produce wealth."

Secular planning (often called "values-based" or "dynasty" planning) assumes that as much wealth as possible should be transferred to the children—and that it will be good for them. Those who read the news or understand anything of history will see many examples of squandered inheritances. You see it in the gossip columns, as well: celebrities' children or grandchildren running around making fools of themselves. It has happened in family after family, including many that are less visible to the public eye.

Traditional planning buys into the illusion that we can manage people over multiple generations, "in perpetuity." I do not believe that we can control other people in that way from beyond the grave. At some level, we can maintain a certain level of control over them while they are living in the same household, but that time will pass. We certainly can continue to have an influence on them, and that can be supported through properly structured estate planning and heir preparation. Even then, however, a significant influence is likely to continue for only two or three generations.

If you were to pass your wealth down to multiple generations in a "dynasty trust" or some other method, do you feel confident that those descendants many generations removed from you would be good stewards of it in a way that honors God? If not, then you might not want to leave your wealth in a structure that passes it on over a long period of time. In other words, a fault of traditional planning is the time frame. "In perpetuity" means for eternity, but everything in this world system must end.

Biblical stewardship takes a different perspective. The only way to continue your resources in perpetuity is to invest in what truly will last for eternity—that is, God's Kingdom, His word, and the souls of men. Instead of simply providing for the comfort, security, and leisure of the future family members many generations removed, biblical stewardship looks to the higher purpose of building a thriving family. At the end of the day, isn't that what you want: a thriving family (not a "lazy family")?

That is why, in your family legacy and inheritance plan, you should carefully consider how much is enough for your children and grandchildren and how much influence over them is appropriate—and then give the rest back to the Owner as an investment in His eternal Kingdom. That way, you build a family that has inspiration, integrity, and initiative. Yours will be a family with a strong work ethic and lasting purpose that includes giving back to society through philanthropy and compassionate, grace-filled charity. It will be a family that seeks to "love God and love others" as ambassadors of the King of Kings.

ARE WE JUST BUILDING "BIGGER BARNS" OR BUILDING GOD'S KINGDOM?

We read in I Timothy 6:6–8 (ESV): "But godliness with contentment is great gain, for we brought nothing into the world, and we cannot take anything out of the world. But if we have food and clothing, with these we will be content."

In stewarding our resources, Christians should look first for God's will, not to the lure of Madison Avenue and Hollywood that strive to make us discontent. Again, we should ask those central questions: How much is appropriate for our lifestyle? How much is enough to leave for our heirs? What does the Lord want us to do with the rest to help a lost, dying, and hurting world that desperately needs Jesus Christ?

At Stewardship Legacy Coaching, we believe God has a better way for us to build a lasting family legacy. We believe in transferring wisdom along with wealth and in preparing the children and grandchildren to be people of virtue and character so that they can be trustworthy stewards of the Lord's resources.

This is how Michael King, vice president and gift planning attorney for the National Christian Foundation, describes our mission:

The incorporation of a biblical worldview perspective should not be taken lightly. It is the key ingredient that makes Stewardship Legacy Coaching and their approach to serving affluent families radically different from the general marketplace.

Whereas the vast majority of advisors that work with affluent families focus predominantly on helping families to "build bigger barns," Stewardship Legacy Coaching encourages families to determine the reasons and purposes for which God has entrusted them with significant wealth, and to use such resources in a much broader way: to appropriately provide for their families; to serve their fellow man, and ultimately to further the building of the Kingdom of God.

In this respect, Stewardship Legacy Coaching takes a much broader view and understanding of "wealth" to include not only a family's financial resources but also their human and intellectual capital, as well as their social capital (what they give back to their community and fellow man.)

It begins with the whispers to the heart as God moves people to do more to show their love for Him by serving others. We work with people to preserve their wealth so that their social capital goes not to taxation, but gets converted to Kingdom Capital.

Sorry, Mr. Franklin, but neither death nor taxes is inevitable, and it is the Christian mission to impact eternity.

For more information and resources about navigating the questions of "how much is enough" and what is an appropriate inheritance, please visit our website at www. stewardshiplegacy.com/resources.

CHAPTER 6 QUESTIONS TO CONSIDER

1. How confident are you that your current plan is a Zero Estate Tax Plan, meaning that the taxes haven't just been minimized (or paid through life insurance) but have actually been eliminated? If you are not 100 percent confident; wouldn't you like to be?

2. As you consider the almost unknown "Gotcha Tax," the IRD (Income in Respect of the Decedent) on 401(k), IRA, and other retirement plan assets, do you have a plan to eliminate the IRD tax on your 401(k) and IRAs (most people don't)?

3. Is your current Estate Plan more like the "fool's plan" in the Bible, just building "bigger barns," or does your plan appropriately provide for your children and grandchildren in a way that is healthy and would avoid "affluenza," while also doing good for your community, making the world a better place and investing in eternity?

SECTION FOUR

BUSINESS LEGACY

CHAPTER 7

BUSINESS AS AN ENGINE OF BLESSING

But seek first the kingdom of God and His righteousness,
and all these things will be added to you.

—Matthew 6:33 (ESV)

For many families that have thrived on the entrepreneurial spirit, their business is the largest asset on their net worth statement. It is their largest investment, producing more income and growth than anything else. And for many business owners (and their spouses), it also provides a sense of identity and a feeling of control.

As we make our way through our few seasons on earth, however, it's hard to support the notion that we are truly in control. Under God's sovereignty, things happen that are beyond our control. We do not control the economy, we do not control the weather, and we do not control other people. We certainly want to exert our influence for good, but many hard-driving entrepreneurial people have a perception of control that really is an illusion.

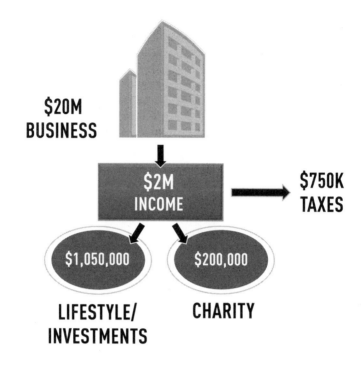

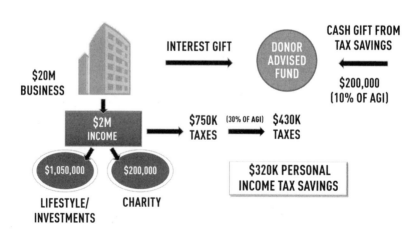

God, however, is eternally and sovereignly in control. The best we can do is submit to Him in our earthly lives as we build toward a future that will be pleasing to Him. In previous chapters, we have looked closely at the various angles of leaving a legacy. Now let's look at what business owners can do to leave their mark on their community and the world in a way that passes on eternal values. Let's consider how a business owner (steward) can transfer wisdom along with the wealth and, in the meantime, use their business as an "Engine of Blessing"!

In chapter 7, we will look at how to instill wisdom in the next generation of business leaders. These are among the concepts we will examine:

- God really owns your business. Think of yourself as His Chief Stewardship Officer.

- The "soft issues" of relationships, values, and faith are as important as the "hard issues" (legal, tax, and financial) involved in business succession or transfer.

- If you are a Christian and a business owner, you should be a Christian business owner. Your faith must extend beyond Sundays.

- Your business can be a platform for Jesus, influencing employees, clients, customers, vendors, and your community for good and for eternity!

HOW ONE FAMILY SAVED A BUSINESS

In chapter 6, I introduced you to a third-generation family business that was able to redirect a large amount of money in estate taxes to worthy causes. We looked at the wealth transfer aspects of that family's business legacy and estate planning. Let's revisit that family now to see how we dealt with the wisdom transfer aspects of their business.

Family and leadership team dynamics are always a critical part of business succession planning. In this particular case, the heir apparent was the business owner's brother. The owner's wife, however, didn't trust her brother-in-law and would never want to be in business with him. Most of the key managers also considered him unqualified and believed his work ethic and values didn't line up with the values for which the family and business had become well known.

This was a situation in which the brother's takeover of the business, if that were allowed to happen, would likely have led to a family feud. The business probably would have failed, not just for wealth transfer reasons but because of difficult family dynamics and the lack of alignment in values.

Through much hard work and gentle, godly counsel involving numerous parties, we were able to help the family (and business) create a plan that would:

- Create a leadership team that would include the brother-in-law, another family member, key managers, and an unbiased third party

- Set up a system of checks and balances for business governance

- Involve the current owner in a plan to instill in the next generation of business leaders, through mentoring and discipleship, the wisdom, values, and life lessons he has learned, the goodwill he has with customers and vendors, and his vision for the culture and mission of the business.

The business owner was challenged to switch gears from focusing primarily on day-to-day operations to making the stewardship of his business legacy a priority. A plan was developed for him to begin to pursue his opportunity to speak into the lives of his brother, the key management team, his children, and the nephews and nieces who also would be involved in the business. He prepared to effectively hand off the baton of stewardship and leadership to the next generation of business leaders

A HARD LOOK AT "SOFT" ISSUES

Sometimes the concepts of wisdom transfer, values alignment, and preparing and mentoring the next generation are referred to as the "soft" issues. Many financial advisors, attorneys, CPAs, and even succession specialists focus instead on the "hard" issues of wealth transfer: the legal, tax, and financial strategies. However, unless the "people issues" get as much attention as the technical issues, those strategies are likely to be ineffective.

Effective stewardship of a business legacy requires a vision and the ability to communicate the mission and values throughout the organization. It has many similarities to family legacy planning. In fact, the business is like another member of the family. It takes careful planning to make sure that the business doesn't ruin the family and that the family doesn't ruin the business. The main difference between family and business legacy planning is that the business legacy involves issues of continuity, exit, and succession planning and various other technical and legal aspects.

> It takes careful planning to make sure that the business doesn't ruin the family and that the family doesn't ruin the business.

The business owner needs to think through these issues because a lack of planning can end up destroying both the business and family legacies. Consider the case of Joe Robbie, the entrepreneur who, in 1965, cofounded the Miami Dolphins, which became one of the most successful teams in professional football. In 1972 the Dolphins had the only perfect season ever in the history of the National Football League. Robbie and his family enjoyed the blessings of that business venture and decided to build a stadium. They named it Joe Robbie Stadium.

Like many owners of family-run businesses, Robbie planned to have his family follow in his footsteps when he was gone. Unfortunately, Robbie never planned to deal with estate taxes and he never thought through all the issues related to his business legacy. When Robbie died in 1990, the stadium and the Miami Dolphins franchise passed to his wife through the marital deduction. When his wife passed away soon after, a split among his nine children and a staggering estate tax bill estimated at $47 million forced the cash-poor family to sell Robbie's legacy, both the football team and the stadium.

That is an example of a legacy lost. Can you imagine being one of the children or grandchildren of Joe Robbie? When you were growing up, you were treated like royalty whenever you walked into the stadium. You watched the games sitting in the VIP booth next to your dad or grandfather. You got to meet the ballplayers and the celebrities. Now, if you go to a game, you are just like anyone else. No VIP booth. No royal treatment. It could have been so different. Had the family pursued a wise strategy, you might have been a new owner of this great team and the stadium might still have continued to carry your family name.

The Robbies could have employed legal, tax, and financial strategies to keep the family business *in* the family. And along with those wealth transfer aspects, the family could have made sure to pass along the wisdom and values as well so that the children might have worked together as a family to preserve their family legacy.

Among their several options, the Robbies could have created a family limited partnership or a family limited LLC and used discount valuation to transfer shares of ownership to family members while Joe was still alive, continuing to do that progressively over time. Or the Robbies could have purchased a $50 million second-to-die life insurance policy to pay the estate taxes. It would have cost about $700,000 a year, which sounds like a lot of money, but compare that with $47 million in taxes. It would have been a small price to pay to keep a multi-million-dollar business in the family.

Another option, and one used by many of our business owner clients, is to create a family foundation and make a substantial charitable gift of the shares of your business to the foundation while you are alive, and even more so upon your death, while allowing the family to maintain control. You could even work it out so that the business would go to the foundation at your death, thereby avoiding all the taxes, and then the family could buy the business back from the charity in an arms-length transaction, following all the appropriate rules.

One method would be to repurchase on an installment note or utilize a wealth replacement trust funded with tax-free cash from life insurance. Another way to deal with the estate tax and still keep the business in the family would have been to use a Zeroed-Out Charitable Lead Annuity Trust (CLAT) or laddered Testamentary Charitable Lead Annuity Trusts (TCLATs). Using these strategies, your money goes to your favorite ministries and charities instead of to the IRS, but your family still ends up owning the business. It's more money for charity, more money for the family, and the family legacy is preserved, which in Joe's case would have kept the Miami Dolphins football team in the family and the Joe Robbie name on the stadium. Family legacy lost. Business legacy lost. Don't let that happen to your family and your business!

Such strategies are not just for the mega-affluent. People of more modest wealth can benefit from them too. Which strategies to use will depend upon the needs of each family, its unique circumstances and goals, the makeup of its assets, and so on. There are many other strategies besides these few that I have mentioned, and we are not recommending any in particular. The main points that we want to make here are:

- Estate taxes are optional (for those who use effective wealth transfer strategies to avoid them).

- Zero Estate Tax Planning can help you keep your family business(es) in your family.

> ## You don't have to let the government "kill the goose that lays the golden eggs."

- You don't have to let the government "kill the goose that lays the golden eggs."

- To create a successful business legacy, you must combine both effective wealth transfer strategies with intentional wisdom transfer, training, and preparing the next generation of business leaders and stewards.

- As in an Olympic relay race, if you drop the "baton" in the handoff to the next generation, you will have failed in the stewardship of your business legacy.

- As does an Olympic athlete, you need a coach, a Family Legacy Coach.

In the same way that family legacy planning involves preparing the next generation in the family, business legacy planning involves preparing the next generation of business leaders. Those leaders may include family members but also will likely include key employees. The owner's responsibility is to figure out how to transfer a lifetime of wisdom—some of it learned through the school of hard knocks—into the next generation of leaders/stewards, as well as to transfer the values upon which the business was built. The aim of that transfer of wisdom is to take care of both the family and the business. Those needs must be balanced.

KEEPING THE FAITH

If you have built a strong Christian culture for which your business is known, how do you prepare the next generation of leaders to perpetuate those same values and culture? How will you be a good steward who makes sure that new chapters are written in the story of your business?

The first step is to integrate your faith throughout your business. When I moved from New England to Florida back in 1987, I often heard Christian business people say, "Oh, that's just business." For them, He was God on Sunday but not from Monday through Friday. What a tragedy! If you are a Christian and a business owner, you should be a *Christian business owner*, which means you understand that the true Owner is God. You may be his Chief Stewardship Officer or Chief Investment Officer, but you are not really the owner. He is.

A lot of good resources teach how to integrate faith and biblical principles into running a business. In addition to classic works such as *Business by the Book* by Larry Burkett and *Business God's Way* by Howard Dayton, organizations such as the C12 Group, Fellowship of Companies for Christ International (FCCI), Convene, Christian Business Men's Connection (CBMC), and others, provide training, resources, and peer accountability. The C12 Group also has a key leaders group where your next-generation leaders can learn and apply biblical business principles along with you. What a great opportunity for you and the leaders you are mentoring!

You should use your business as a platform to influence employees, clients, customers, vendors, and your community. As a Christian, you should be an ambassador of Jesus Christ in your unique sphere of influence, which includes your business. A good ambassador acts as a statesman does. Your business can be a platform for Christ if you choose to use it that way.

We are meant to be more than simply containers of money from generation to generation. Your business can be a conduit for Kingdom Capital. If God has blessed your business with good cash flow and profits beyond the needs of your family and employees, what will you do with that excess? Will you just be building bigger barns and living a life of increasing consumption and materialism? Or will you use those resources as a conduit for God's Kingdom?

CONTAINER vs CONDUIT

We will take a closer look in the next chapter at what business owners should do, and we also have resources about the stewardship of your business legacy on our website at www.StewardshipLegacy.com/business.

CHAPTER 7 QUESTIONS TO CONSIDER

1. Do you have a plan to use your business as a platform for Christ by creating a caring culture for your employees, customers, and others in your spheres of influence?

2. Are you currently using your business as an "engine of blessing" to invest in God's Kingdom?

3. What would you like your business legacy to look like, and what has to happen to help assure that will happen?

4. Do you have well thought out, written, and communicated Business Continuity and Succession Plans?

5. Have you selected the next "stewards/leaders" for your business and do you have a plan to effectively equip them with the wisdom and skills they will need to build upon the business foundation you have laid. The future of your business and your legacy depend on it!

CHAPTER 8

HANDING OFF THE BATON

Do you see a man skilled in his work? He will stand
before kings; He will not stand before obscure men.

—Proverbs 22:29 (NASB)

So many business owners, when they get to a certain stage in life, realize that they are not going to be able to run the business forever. Sometimes they have just gotten tired of it or tired of the stress and pressure. They want to sell so that they can retire, relax, and enjoy life. Sometimes they want to quit the business because they are facing health issues. For whatever reason, they realize they will not be keeping their hands on the helm forever.

It is then that the business owner begins to struggle with a variety of concerns that come down to this question: "How can I efficiently and effectively transfer the business so that I can be confident that my spouse and I will have enough money for the rest of our lives while also making sure the business is in good hands so that we can feel good about our legacy?"

In chapter 8, we will examine a few of the many questions and some solutions for business owners who are preparing to sell or transition their life's work to new ownership, often to the next generation. We will look at considerations such as these:

- Wisely stewarding the largest financial transaction of your life

- Structuring the deal wisely to minimize tax consequences

- Distributing the estate fairly if not all the children are interested in the business

- Avoiding sibling rivalries that can kill a business

- Balancing the ICE of income, control, and equity

- Developing a business continuity, growth, and exit plan

- Preparing the next generation of business leaders

A GOOD DEAL FOR ALL

For many business owners, the sale or transfer of the business will be the largest single financial transaction of their lives. As one of their biggest risks and greatest opportunities, this transaction must be stewarded wisely so that it can become a good and fair deal for all: the seller, the buyer, the next generation if it stays in the family, and for the business itself so that it still has the resources to thrive.

> For many business owners, the sale or transfer of the business will be the largest single financial transaction of their lives.

Unfortunately, most business owners and their advisors are not proactive and intentional in their planning. The planning often starts too late, sometimes not until an offer has been accepted, and by then, many good strategies are off the table. As a result, most businesses owners end up paying a large amount in capital gains and income taxes that could have been avoided.

In many cases, the owners, by wisely structuring the sale, using both charitable and noncharitable strategies, can save tens or hundreds of thousands of dollars and often millions in taxes. If that money had not gone to the government, they could have put it to such uses as these:

- Securing their own financial future and paying for goals in their next phase of life, such as travel, visiting the grandchildren, or charitable pursuits

- More resources, if appropriate, as an inheritance for the children and grandchildren

- More generous contributions to causes and organizations that make a difference in their community, in the world, and for eternity

As they contemplate retiring or exiting, business owners also wonder how to equitably distribute the estate among the children, since one or more may be involved in running the business while others are not. Just because a child has no interest or lacks the skills to work in the family business does not mean that he or she does not have an interest in the wealth created by the business.

On the other hand, you don't want a situation in which a child who knows nothing about the business can tell a brother or sister who is running it what to do. The children often can have competing priorities and conflicting values. A child who is not employed in the business may be primarily concerned with getting dividends and cash flow from his or her shares, for example, while the child who runs the business may want to reinvest in it, buy new equipment, expand into new markets, grow the company and take advantage of opportunities—all of which requires capital. To succeed, a business transition plan must be structured to avoid such sibling rivalry that could kill the business.

Beyond the personal and family concerns, the owners at the same time need to leave the business with enough resources to allow it to remain profitable for the new owners, whether they are the children, key employees, or others. After all, it represents their life's work, and they are proud of it, and they want it to continue to serve the community and to give back to mankind and to God's Kingdom. In fact, the ongoing success of the business is part of their legacy.

ICE: INCOME, CONTROL, EQUITY

As business owners consider how to plan for their exit and succession, they generally face three big issues, represented by the acronym ICE. It stands for income, control, and equity.

The owners want to know whether they will have enough income to retire comfortably and whether sufficient income still will be flowing into the business once they no longer are there. They wonder whether the business can produce enough income for all parties involved. They also are thinking about control issues. How can the control of the business properly be transitioned to the next generation? Should they give up control all at once or gradually? Will the new leaders be able to run the business well on their own? In addition, business owners are concerned about transfer of equity, or ownership: How can that be accomplished smoothly and fairly and with minimum taxation?

Over the years, I have seen many business owners who are still working hard even in their seventies and eighties and are unwilling to give up control. Their reason? They don't trust how the next generation would run the business. But one day they will have to take their hand off the helm, and then what?

Business owners have other concerns, as well, that can stop them from handing off the baton effectively. As they exit, they not only need an income, but also a way to maintain their identity apart from the business. They will have many more hours of free time each day. How will they use that extra time? This is a great opportunity to become involved in ministry and other volunteer activities. It's a good time to finally take up that long-postponed hobby. And it's a good time to get to know the children and grandchildren better than ever, spend time with friends, travel, and see the beauty of God's creation. It's important to have a plan for using that time.

The prospective successors, whether it's the children or key employees, also have concerns. They need to assume control so they can do their job without undue interference. The founder should not continue to control the business or micromanage successors as an "absentee owner."

Beyond the issues of income and control are equity and ownership issues. Neither control of the business nor the equity shares need to be divided equally, and they seldom are. Instead, the equity and control should be divided *equitably*, meaning appropriately and fairly, which is not necessarily the same as equally. Ron Blue's principle that we mentioned in chapter 4 holds true here: "We need to love our children equally, but we need to treat them uniquely."

One ingenious way of dealing with the issues of income, control, and equity, whether at the founder level or the level of the children or key employees, involves balancing those three issues. This method allows the first generation to maintain income and control while beginning to transfer (or sell) the equity ownership via a gradual, well-planned transition.

That often can be accomplished by recapitalizing the company (an LLC, an S or C corporation, or a partnership) into managing and nonmanaging shares. The current business owners can progressively sell or transfer some of the nonmanaging shares to the children, key employees, or business partners. The owners are not giving up control because they still own the managing shares. Shares can often be transferred to family members on a discounted valuation basis through numerous structures including family trusts, intentionally defective irrevocable grantor trusts (IDGTs), family limited partnerships, family limited liability companies, and so on.

Nonmanaging shares can also be gifted to charity through a donor-advised fund or family foundation, while producing significant tax deductions to help offset the taxes that would otherwise have been paid on the sale. One organization calls this a charitable shareholder strategy; another calls it business as an engine of blessing. By any name, the strategy is wise stewardship.

Often, through wise structuring of the sale with both noncharitable and charitable strategies, the owners can, personally, net more. Yes, they can actually make a profit by giving some of it away! In doing so, they also can bless their children and grandchildren, and money that would otherwise have been paid in taxes can now be redirected to the ministries and causes they care deeply about. It's a win-win-win.

PREPARING FOR THE EXIT

Business owners often wonder when they should begin to prepare for their exit. They may be unsure how they will go about handing over the reins and what they should do to make the business as attractive as possible for a potential buyer and to increase the valuation of the business. They often are unsure of just how much the business is worth and whether it will give them enough to live the lifestyle they envision in the next phase of their lives.

We recommend starting with what we call a business continuity plan, which is different from a business succession plan or exit plan. The continuity plan is like the instructions for a pilot in an emergency. In other words, by definition, the business continuity plan is not the perfect succession plan but, rather, one that spells out who would run the business and how things would get done if the plan needed to be implemented tomorrow. It's a stopgap or contingency plan so that the business could carry on if the owner were to die or become disabled suddenly and unexpectedly. A business continuity plan is flexible and can easily be updated as circumstances change.

We then develop a business growth and "value creation" plan to maximize the value of the business and to get all elements of the business operating like clockwork in preparation for the transition. We use a variety of tools, such as an ExitMap™ assessment and a Deep-Dive Analysis that reviews eighteen key value drivers to measure financial, legal, tax, structural, and documentation readiness. These are important elements that influence the valuation multiple and how much the owners could get for the business were they to sell it. We also look at the operational readiness: the people, processes, and systems. Many owners, particularly Christian business owners, also should evaluate values and cultural readiness and look for ways to improve them.

The aim of this growth and "value creation" planning is to get all these things shipshape well before the exit, with a well-functioning team. Buyers pay more when they see value and quality.

The third step is the business succession or exit plan. This is the thorough plan that you would like to have in place if you had the time to implement all the legal, tax, financial, operational, and marketing strategies for effective business transition. It identifies the next generation of business leaders and includes the financial, operational, legal, tax, and marketing aspects of the business, all fully documented.

So much is at stake. Do you know how much value you need to get from the sale or transition of your business to secure financial freedom for yourself and your spouse? Will the amount you receive after taxes be sufficient? The answers to those questions and more can all be wrapped up in a well-drafted business succession and exit plan. Most businesses don't have a good one. Does yours?

STEWARDSHIP OF YOUR BUSINESS LEGACY

Most business owners have heard about continuity, succession, and exit planning, but they have heard nothing about planning for the stewardship of their business legacy. They have yet to consider the wisdom transfer that should accompany the wealth transfer aspects in their business transition.

Business legacy planning involves the transfer of the culture and values that define the business. You want to perpetuate the mission and vision, the guiding principles and core values upon which you built the business. Your successors, whether they are key employees or your children, should still hold those values dear as they take the company into the next season.

This is a critical part of your legacy. You must identify and invest in the next generation of business leaders and instill a high level of integrity in them. During the succession process, you need to shift from managing the company to leading it, ensuring that the new leaders integrate your values throughout the culture.

A primary mission of all business owners should be to mentor and disciple the next generation of leaders and stewards who will follow them. They need to learn through education and experience. If you want to make sure that the business will be running well, long after you are gone, nothing is more important than to prepare the person and the team to whom you will pass the baton. This is a great responsibility and opportunity to influence the lives of those around you: the people with whom you have worked for years, the people you love, your friends and colleagues, and whoever will assume your role as the next leader.

A primary mission of all business owners should be to mentor and disciple the next generation of leaders and stewards who will follow them.

To do that effectively, you need a plan to inculcate those values into the DNA of your organization and its leadership. We can help. Through our Thriving Business Legacy™ coaching process, we can create a customized plan to address these crucial matters in a way that fits the unique nature of your business and family needs.

We have been blessed in America with opportunities to build successful businesses. How will you steward the blessings given to you? That is an exciting challenge that transcends the many financial, legal, and tax details involved. The baton is in your hands, ready to be passed to the next generation of stewards. Are they prepared? What will be your business legacy?

CHAPTER 8 QUESTIONS TO CONSIDER

1. For most business owners, their business is by far the largest asset on their Net Worth Statement and for most, the sale or transfer of their business will be the largest single financial transaction of their lives. Do you have a plan to wisely steward that transaction without killing the goose that lays the golden eggs?

2. Do you have a well-thought-out and written Business Continuity Plan so that if you didn't wake up tomorrow, all of the key people (family and business) would know who is going to play what role and would operate as a cohesive team?

3. What are the things that are in your head and in your heart that the next generation of business leaders and stewards would need to know to successfully run the business?

4. Do you have a plan for separating the business of being a family from running the family business so that both your family and your business will not only survive but thrive for generations to come?

SECTION FIVE

KINGDOM LEGACY

CHAPTER 9

LIVING OUT YOUR LEGACY

For what does it profit a man to gain the
whole world and forfeit his soul?

—Mark 8:36 (ESV)

I believe that all human beings want to leave their mark on the world, a legacy that will last beyond their lifetime. The philanthropic spirit, common to all people, reaches out to help our fellow man, both while we are alive and after we are gone. Christians take that to the level of leaving a legacy that will resound throughout eternity. It is much more than financial. It is our Kingdom legacy.

Years ago, I met with a financially blessed couple who had a good offer on the table for the sale of their business. They were looking for a graceful and well-planned exit from those day-to-day responsibilities so that they might spend more time in ministry endeavors and with their children and the grandchildren to come.

The husband was a close advisor to an international missions organization, to which the couple had contributed significantly in recent years. The couple also were generous donors to their church and several other ministries both locally and globally.

As I began working with the couple on their business exit and legacy strategies, the husband talked about their priorities. After selling the business, they, of course, were looking for sufficient income to meet their needs. And then the husband explained that his wife was twelve years younger and likely would outlive him by a few decades. He wanted to leave her enough to live comfortably for the rest of her life, but neither of them knew how much that would require. That lack of clarity and confidence about how much would be enough was holding them back from selling their business and pursuing the life of purpose to which they both felt God was prompting them.

The husband told me he no longer wished to be involved in management but wanted to remain involved in the business by helping to develop strategic relationships and mentoring the next generation of business owners and leaders. He had decided to spend only perhaps a quarter as much time with the business. He now wanted to spend more time using his talents, experience, and wisdom for Kingdom purposes. In addition, the couple wished to travel more, and golf was one of his passions.

As we worked together to consider their Kingdom legacy, we discussed six areas of life, or "the six currencies," that they could wisely steward. Three of them were the stewardship of their *time, talents, and treasure*—often called the three Ts—and stewardship of their *leadership, relationships, and influence*. We each have the potential to steward those six currencies for lifetime impact on the world around us and on eternity.

One of the steps that the husband has taken is to leverage relationships—his spheres of influence and those of others in the ministry—by convening potential donors for golf tournaments. That effort has raised significant sums for God's Kingdom, an eternal return on investment for his time. He was able to incorporate his time, talents, leadership, relationships, and influence into an activity that he and his friends and colleagues enjoyed. Yes, golf and other hobbies can be used for God's Kingdom.

At the same time, his wife has used her gifts, talents, and relationships to set up forums that bring women donors and couples together in a spirit of collaboration. Previously, while the men attended board meetings and golfing events, their wives were less engaged in the fund raising. The wife's influence has helped to create a family atmosphere among the major donors to the ministries they support.

In chapter 9, we will focus on transferring God's wisdom to your children and grandchildren—and that begins with modeling those values day by day. We will consider these truths:

- The work of the Kingdom should begin in your own home and family.

- You can profoundly influence those whom God has put in your life.

- You should wisely steward the six currencies of time, talents, treasure, leadership, relationships, and influence.

- The rising generations are a mission field of priority.

- By living your life authentically, others can see God in you.

IMPACT ON ETERNITY

Our Kingdom legacy is the ultimate investment. It is investing in souls. We can have a tremendous impact on the world around us.

The motto of the extraordinary ministry World Help is "Help for today and hope for tomorrow"—and that is the spirit that drives Christians to reach out with compassion to meet the needs of others less fortunate, both locally and globally. We have opportunities to have an impact on eternity. We can help to feed, clothe, and educate people, meeting their needs for today, and we also can share the good news of Jesus Christ with them, giving them hope for the rest of their lives and for eternity. We can also meet their needs in ways that lead to sustainability, allowing them to help themselves, giving them a hand up, not just a handout. This way we help break the cycle of poverty and also give them the sense of self worth and accomplishment that comes from improving their own situation. This is impact investing: have an impact on others for good. If all we do is help meet their physical and emotional needs but neglect their greatest need, to fill the hole in their soul and to give them the peace of knowing they can spend eternity with the Lord, we will not have met their most important need.

Meeting the needs of those less fortunate and sharing the good news of Jesus Christ has been my passion since I became a Christian as a teenager. Helping others do that through wisely stewarding their time, talents, and treasures as well as their leadership, relationships, and influence is not only my business but also my calling. My career has focused on helping families and business owners become more strategic and intentional with their stewardship and their legacy, first within their own homes and businesses and communities, and then around the globe, through their work with causes that are near and dear to their hearts.

Though there is much work to be done abroad, the work of the Kingdom should begin in our own homes and families. We might do noble works in our community and the world, but what a loss if we have neglected to inspire and influence our own children and grandchildren. In his book *The Man in the Mirror*, Patrick Morley talks about the emptiness of success when our priorities are misaligned. The relationships that matter most are the ones at home.

Billy Sunday experienced that tragedy in his own family. A former major league baseball player, he became a celebrated evangelist in the early 1900s, attracting huge crowds at cities around the nation. He was the Billy Graham of his time. The tabernacle floors in those days were covered with sawdust to muffle the shuffling of thousands of feet and to hold down the dust as thousands came forward at Sunday's invitation to accept Christ. Their answer to the call became known as "hitting the sawdust trail." He was heartbroken, however, by the behavior of his own sons. Late in life, he said he regretted trying to save the whole world while watching his own family go to hell.

When I first heard that account, it shook me to the core. How many Christian families, how many business owners, how many pastors might one day feel such regrets? Our own families, our children and grandchildren, should be our most important mission field. They must not be sacrificed on the altar of ministry or of business or for the almighty dollar. Neglect need not be intentional. We all can get our priorities wrong at times. What's important is to recognize when that happens and turn it around so that we do not someday grieve for what might have been.

> Our own families, our children and grandchildren, should be our most important mission field. They must not be sacrificed on the altar of ministry or of business or for the almighty dollar.

After the family, the next mission field to have our highest priority is our sphere of influence: the extended family, friends, employees, customers, church members, our local community, and whomever else God has put within our reach. They are, in a sense, our "Jerusalem."

ARROWS IN THE QUIVER

Family leaders should involve their children and grandchildren in their charitable giving, teaching them to be generous and to have a heart for their community and the world. Children should see that generosity modeled in their parents and grandparents, as well as see them model a life of serving and biblical stewardship.

"As arrows are in the hands of a mighty man, so are children of the youth. Happy is the man that has his quiver full of them," we read in Psalms 127:4-5 (KJV). As we go through our Stewardship Legacy Coaching process, I like to challenge families to think of their children and grandchildren as the arrows that they can launch to have an impact on eternity. I ask them to focus on guiding children and grandchildren to be the kind of people God wants them to be. That's more than just mentoring; it's truly Intergenerational Discipleship™. Rising generations in your family should become the mission field of your highest priority.

Charles Spurgeon, the great nineteenth-century English Baptist

> As we go through our Stewardship Legacy Coaching process, I like to challenge families to think of their children and grandchildren as the arrows that they can launch to have an impact on eternity.

preacher, spoke about heirs and wealth as he preached on Proverbs 20:7 (AKJV): "The just man walks in his integrity; his children are blessed after him." Here is what he had to say:

> Anxiety about our family is natural, but we shall be wise if we turn it into care about our own character. If we walk before the Lord in integrity, we shall do more to bless our descendants than if we bequeath them large estates. A father's holy life is a rich legacy for his sons.
>
> The upright man leaves his heirs his example, and this in itself will be a mine of true wealth. How many men may trace their success in life to the example of their parents? He leaves them also his repute [reputation]. Men think better of us as the sons of a man who could be trusted, the successors of a tradesman of excellent repute [reputation]. Oh, that all young men were anxious to keep up the family name! Above all, he leaves his children his prayers and the blessing of a prayer-hearing God, and these make our offspring to be favored among the sons of men. God will save them even after we are dead. Oh that they might be saved at once!
>
> Our integrity may be God's means of saving our sons and daughters. If they see the truth of our religion proved by our lives, it may be that they will believe in Jesus for themselves. Lord, fulfill this word to my household!

A father's holy life is a rich legacy for his sons.

As I read Spurgeon's words, I was inspired that this is the type of legacy that godly people should want to leave to their children and their grandchildren. It all begins with our personal legacy, living our own lives with integrity and faith, working hard, and operating with honesty in all that we do. It means living our lives authentically. It means *living faithfully.*

When we are not living what we believe, we cannot successfully pass on a family legacy of faith. Children and grandchildren recognize hypocrisy, and it drives them away from the faith that we hold so dear.

As you think about living out your own legacy, consider the six currencies, including the three Ts:

- How are you using your *time*? Are you devoting enough of it to your own walk with Christ? To your family?

- Are you putting your *talents,* a gift from the Creator, to their fullest and highest use?

- What are you doing with your *treasure*? Where you invest it is where your heart will be.

- Are you demonstrating the level of *leadership* to which you have been called?

- Are you developing *relationships* that will serve God's purposes?

- How could He use you to *influence* the lives of the people who are within your sphere of influence.

Our legacy is much more about our example of godly and authentic living than about the amount of money we leave to our children and grandchildren. Our legacy is something we live out, not something we merely leave behind.

> Our legacy is something we live out, not something we merely leave behind.

CHAPTER 9 QUESTIONS TO CONSIDER

1. Consider the concept of stewarding the six currencies of your time, talents, treasure, leadership, relationships, and influence. Think of one idea involving each of these currencies that you could implement to help others? (Write it down!)

2. How do Spurgeon's words—"If we walk before the Lord in integrity, we shall do more to bless our descendants than if we bequeath them large estates"—affect the way you view your legacy to your children and grandchildren?

3. How does the statement, "Our legacy is something we live out, not something we merely leave behind," affect your approach to "finishing well"?

CHAPTER 10

INVESTING IN ETERNITY

For where your treasure is, there your heart will be also.

—Matthew 6:21 (NIV)

Every one of us, at some point, will die. The ratio, historically, has been 1:1, with only a few exceptions that are well documented in the Bible.

Knowing that, our thoughts must turn to what we will leave behind as our legacy for God's Kingdom. Most of us desire to leave a good, godly, and lasting legacy, but what we leave behind also will include the wealth we have accumulated for a lifetime: our "treasure."

"I have never seen a U-Haul being towed by a hearse," I heard a pastor say many years ago. In other words, you can't take your money with you, but you certainly can "send it on ahead," a point that Randy Alcorn highlights in his wonderful book *The Treasure Principle.* Christians have the potential to invest their resources not just for today, or for the next generation or two, but for eternity. We can leave a Kingdom legacy.

In this chapter, we will see how those of us blessed with more than we need can best put our resources to work as part of our Kingdom legacy. We will consider the following:

- We live in a world of desperate needs

- With our resources, we can provide help for today

- As Christians, we can also provide hope for tomorrow

- Even small steps can transform lives

- How to create capital for the Kingdom

"HELP FOR TODAY AND HOPE FOR TOMORROW"

In my small community outside Orlando, Florida, my church has a "buses n' backpacks" ministry. In 2017 the ministry gave more than 80,000 meals to poor children and their families. At the Orlando Union Rescue Mission and rescue missions around the nation, people who are homeless and hungry can get both a good meal and the good news of Jesus Christ.

Organizations with a global reach work to feed, clothe, and educate people. Among the many good groups are World Help, Samaritan's Purse, Compassion International, World Vision, and World Relief. A ministry called Opportunity International is involved in microenterprise efforts to help people in Third World countries start small businesses so that they might provide for their own families. This organization does more than give people fish to feed them for a day. It teaches them to fish so that they can feed themselves for a lifetime.

As we avail ourselves of such opportunities to provide help for today, we also have the opportunity to provide hope for tomorrow through the power of Jesus Christ to change lives. Many non-Christian efforts are also tirelessly dedicated to relief, and they are worthy of praise, but we believe that people also are hungry and thirsty in their souls. They are looking for hope for tomorrow, not just help for today. We believe in helping the whole person—physically, emotionally, intellectually, and spiritually.

The world has no shortage of people who are starving, hurting, and without hope. Many of our clients focus on Kingdom investments that will have an impact on situations that are heartbreaking. The issues are nearly endless: poverty, illiteracy, social injustice, unclean water, disease, natural disasters, sex trafficking, and many others. If we have been blessed with more than we need, we must ask how we can best be stewards of those resources, not just our treasure, but our time and talents as well.

Using our leadership, relationships, and influence, we can we roll up our sleeves and get involved in the causes that are near and dear to our hearts. Consider what your own family can do. Let your children and grandchildren see firsthand the desperate needs of others. That experience will help them become more compassionate about the needs of others and more grateful for what they've been blessed with. As Todd Harper, the president of Generous Giving, has said, "I've never met an unhappy, generous person." Giving not only blesses others, it brings joy to our lives as well. As Jesus said, "It is more blessed to give than to receive," and I think Jesus knew something about giving and living the blessed life!

WHO IS YOUR AMY JO?

As I was writing this chapter, I read a Facebook post from a young person who works in Orlando. This story demonstrates how each of us might make a difference by using our time, talents, and treasures as well as our leadership, relationships, and influence. Here is an abridged version of the post:

> Each day for a week, I saw Amy Jo at a corner in downtown Orlando, and she never asked for money. She simply said, "Good morning, sir, have a great day. God bless!" and smiled. Every Tuesday, she and I now have lunch together. I get to hear how positive she is, though she really has nothing.

> Last week Amy Jo dropped a bomb on me: she cannot read. Amy Jo does not smoke, drink, have a drug addiction, or anything of that nature. She simply just has never had anyone teach her how to read. She told me how hard it was to find work, not being able to read. She told me that any money that she can collect, she uses to buy books that help with learning to read instead of buying food.

> This crushed me! I have been blessed with a family that has always had resources to provide me with anything I wanted. Amy Jo has not. So now I'm teaching her to read. I check out one library book a week and we read it together on Tuesdays, and she practices on her own the rest of the week.

> There are a lot of people out there like Amy Jo, and not all are hungry, homeless, or hurt. Some could be your family or friends. Helping someone could be as easy as saying

hello and smiling. You never know what you can do for someone until you try.

Who is your Amy Jo?

A week later, the young person reported that Amy Jo had been able to check in to a hotel, thanks to an outpouring of generosity from the community. People have been trying to arrange permanent accommodation for her and offering her groceries, clothes, and other donations. The young person is now arranging to set up a foundation in her name to help other homeless people in the area.

The spirit of reaching out, it would seem, is alive and well. This is just one example of how, through the stewardship of our resources, we can help to change the world, one life at a time. We can make a difference in our communities and throughout the world. Though we might start out with small steps, our impact can become transformational. Our influence can be life-changing—and eternity changing. If you want to do this in a way that transforms your own family, involve your children and grandchildren in reaching out and serving those less fortunate. Make it a family affair!

CREATING KINGDOM CAPITAL

As we help others, we must first provide the immediate resources to meet their urgent needs. That's the foundation to build trusting relationships that give us the credibility and opportunity to share the good news of Jesus Christ and meet the eternal needs of their soul.

One way to provide help for today and hope for tomorrow is to convert money that we otherwise would pay in taxes and use it for charitable and philanthropic purposes. In other words, we can Convert Our Social Capital into Kingdom Capital™.

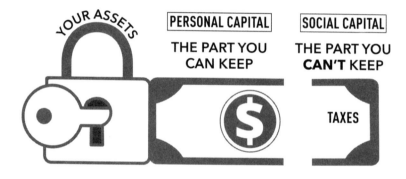

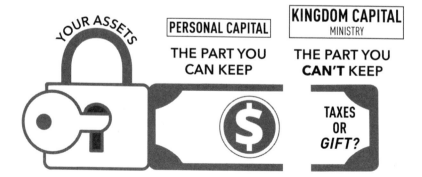

In doing so, we can focus on "asset-based giving" instead of just giving cash. Statistics from the National Christian Foundation show that 91 percent of all the wealth owned by Americans is in the form of assets such as real estate, stocks, a closely held business, and investments in a 401(k). Only 9 percent of the wealth is in the form of cash. And yet it is through cash that people give 90 percent of their donations to charitable causes. In other words, charities are depending on that small sliver of wealth (cash) as the source for almost all the giving.

We need to unlock those non-cash elements of our wealth so they can be used more widely for charitable and Kingdom purposes. Not only can we increase the flow to charity, but the tax advantages to us can be quite advantageous. Some people, for example, give from their investment portfolio. If you donate highly appreciated stocks or mutual funds, you get the same tax deduction as if it were cash, but at the same time you can avoid the substantial capital gains tax that you would otherwise have paid on those appreciated securities. Likewise, if you are selling real estate that you bought years ago for, say, $100,000, and that is now worth $1 million, you will be facing a capital gains tax on the $900,000 of growth in value. However, if you give some of that real estate away prior to the sale—and it must be *prior* to the sale—you avoid that capital gains tax on the portion you donate and you also get a tax deduction for your gift.

In a similar manner, if you own a business you can make God a partner in it by giving shares of the business to charitable causes. You then have some of that Schedule K-1 income or profits from your business flowing directly, every year, to your own donor-advised fund or family foundation. From there, you can distribute the money to the causes that you care about, saving a lot of money in taxes. In fact, it is possible, in many cases, to increase your personal cash flow through this type of asset-based charitable giving. We often help our clients accomplish this.

WHAT ASSETS ARE *OWNED?*

91%

■ CASH

■ OTHER ASSETS

WHAT ASSETS ARE *GIVEN?*

94%

91% of all assets owned are **NOT** cash assets, but are other assets.

94% of all gifts are gifts of cash.

Thus, of all charitiable gifts made,94% comes from the 9% of assets that are CASH assets

I point out these few examples because they represent many such opportunities to give back to the community, the world, and to the Kingdom of the God who created us. There is much you can do with your time, talents, and treasures, and with your leadership, relationships, and influence.

THE THREE HUGS

Let me share something I learned from a longtime mentor and friend, Ray Lyne, founder of Lifestyle Giving. I consider Ray, a wonderful man of God, to be the grandfather of Christian estate design and planned giving.

There are three hugs, he told me, to a good legacy plan. You will know that you have had great success if:

- Your children are still hugging each other six months after you die

- When you get to heaven, people hug you because you helped them to get there, either by personally

CONCLUSION

ONLY ONE LIFE

Now if anyone builds on the foundation with gold, silver, precious
stones, wood, hay, straw—each one's work will become manifest,
for the Day will disclose it, because it will be revealed by fire,
and the fire will test what sort of work each one has done. If the
work that anyone has built on the foundation survives, he will
receive a reward. If anyone's work is burned up, he will suffer
loss, though he himself will be saved, but only as through fire.

—1 Corinthians 3:12–15 (ESV)

Early in my career, I had an experience with a client that gripped me to the core. Ever since, I have been determined to try to help as many people as I can to be intentional and proactive about building a strong and lasting family and business legacy.

I'll call him Al. It's not his real name, and I won't identify his successful business except to say that most people would recognize it. Al had come to me for financial planning, and we had developed a good relationship. He sought my advice on a variety of planning, investment, tax, business, and estate matters. We talked about how to best manage his business for growth and how to wisely create a holistic plan for his family and finances.

Al did not come from a faith perspective. Though he had made millions and had many material trappings, he was deeply frustrated with his family relationships and his marriage. He talked to me about the emptiness of his "success" and what money had produced in his life. His family was a mess. He had only the business and the money.

"Jeff, you are my best friend in the world," he told me once, which broke my heart because it simply wasn't so. We were not particularly close. We had a good relationship as client and advisor, but for Al to consider me his best friend in the world meant that he didn't have any friends at all.

Often, our business conversations would gravitate toward his personal and family life, his disappointments and frustrations. He told me that his marriage had been virtually nonexistent for over thirty years and that his relationship with his adult daughter was strained.

"The only thing in my life that works for me is doing business and making money," he told me. "The rest of my life is a shambles."

I shared with him some of the principles we've discussed throughout this book and the importance of making his family a higher priority than his business or making money. I also shared the good news of Jesus Christ with him. We talked about how he needed to know the Lord and to know God's higher plan and purpose for his life. We had that kind of conversation numerous times. Al looked forward to those conversations and acknowledged that what I was saying was true, and yet he never was willing to surrender the grip that money and "success" had on his life. He was not ready to surrender to a higher purpose and a higher power.

Over the years, Al became disenchanted with the business and had an opportunity to sell it. He sought my counsel, and I advised him against selling the business for a number of reasons. I knew that it was pretty much his whole source of identity, but selling it also didn't make sense from a financial perspective. His business was a cash cow and generated significant cash flow, and the multiple that he could get from a sale just wouldn't justify it.

"Instead of selling," I suggested, "perhaps you can hire somebody to run the business on your behalf, give that person a six-figure salary and some of the equity or profits, and you could be a nonmanaging owner and be freed up from the day-to-day operations. You can enjoy life but still have the business and the income it provides."

But against my advice, Al sold the business with the dream of retiring, playing golf, and traveling. And for the first few months, that's what he did. He played golf almost every day, bought drinks for everybody at the nineteenth hole, and seemed to be enjoying himself. His old business associates would hang around with him so long as he was buying.

Eventually, though, he grew tired of all that golfing, and frankly, his personality was so abrasive that he drove people away. That's what he had done with his family, that's what he did in business, and that's what he was doing in retirement. In fact, I'd had my doubts that I would be able to continue working with such a difficult individual, but I had come to care about him as a person and felt that God had me in his life for a reason.

One day, about four or five months after Al retired, I was on my way to the office from a morning appointment when I got a call from my staff. "Jeff, you need to get here as soon as possible," one of my colleagues told me. "Al is here. And he looks like he's on the verge of suicide."

By the time I got to my office, Al had left. I tried to track him down, calling all his phone numbers. Eventually, I reached him and persuaded him to come back to the office so that we could talk. He returned later that day.

"Jeff, what have I done?" he asked me. "I've sold my baby. I never should have sold the company. You told me not to, but I did it anyway, and I've sold my baby! It was the only thing in my life that worked, and now she's gone." Al continued to lament his decision. He called it the biggest mistake of his life. Not only was it a financial mistake, he said, but he no longer had a reason to live. He felt hopeless.

I reminded him, first, that he had money that he could redeploy and invest in other ventures. He had built businesses successfully before, so he could do it again, I told him. But most importantly, I shared with him the importance of finding his higher purpose and getting to know the Purpose Giver, Jesus Christ.

This was not news to Al. We had talked about the Good News numerous times, and I had shared with him *The Four Spiritual Laws* by the late Bill Bright, founder of Campus Crusade for Christ.

FOUR SPIRITUAL LAWS

1. God loves you and offers a wonderful plan for your life.

2. Man is sinful and separated from God. Therefore, he cannot know and experience God's love and plan for his life.

3. Jesus Christ is God's only provision for our sin. Through him alone we can know God personally and experience God's love and plan.

4. We must individually receive Jesus Christ as Savior and Lord; then we can know and experience God's love and plan for our lives.

"I am beyond hope," Al said to me on that day. "You don't know what I've done. You don't know what evil and wickedness I've done in my life. I am beyond the reach of even God." I explained that God's grace can reach anybody and is greater than all our sins. I offered a number of scripture verses and emphasized his need for Christ.

We were there for hours in my office, from midmorning into the evening. For part of that time, Al was on his hands and knees, crawling around the conference room floor, lamenting his hopelessness. I was reminded of Nebuchadnezzar in the Old Testament, who for seven years grazed on the grass like a cow. As Al was weeping in torment on the floor, it was clear to both of us that he had lost his identity and sense of purpose for living. He had no sense of belonging, no hope. It truly did feel to him as if he had lost his baby, his life, his reason for living.

With Al's permission, I asked my staff to reach out to his wife, and she came in. She was a Christian and pleaded with her husband to make Jesus the Lord and Savior of his life. She told him that he was not beyond hope and that there still was hope for their marriage, and for their daughter and grandchild. The grace that could have been his for all eternity was within his reach, but he kept resisting it out of his belief that he was beyond hope.

As I talked with Al throughout that day, I felt confident that he would come to trust Christ. After all, my experience had always been that all those with whom I had shared the Gospel received Christ as their Savior. I would like to tell you that by the end of the day, Al did too. But that is not how the story ends. By seven o'clock that night, when he left the office to go home, he had not surrendered. He left with the same depth of hopelessness and despair with which he had come in.

I tried to reach out to Al for a number of months after that. Most of the time, he was not willing to meet or to talk. Many times, I would leave a message with his wife. On those occasions when Al and I did speak, I tried each time to share the good news and to challenge him to find that higher purpose and to find the Purpose Giver. Eventually, he shut off communications and would not take my calls or return them, and he made it clear that he did not want me to visit their home.

Al's relationship with his wife continued to deteriorate. He took up residence on the second floor, while his wife and their daughter and grandchild lived on the first floor. Al would not leave the house for any reason, and he would not come downstairs. He would not shower, shave, or cut his fingernails. He would not come down even to eat. Had his wife not taken food to him, I suspect he might have starved. When I last saw Al, he looked like Howard Hughes in his later days.

"WHOEVER LOVES MONEY ..."

That was all years ago, and yet I still think about Al and pray for him. I believe we would all agree that this was a lost opportunity for a personal, family, and business legacy that might have resounded through eternity. In fact, I think we would all agree that this was a tragedy.

I learned some valuable lessons. I learned how crucial it is that people have a purpose for living that is beyond their business and making money and playing golf with a few drinking buddies, and beyond the material trappings of this world. People need the Purpose Giver. He is needed in the most impoverished villages. He is needed in the boardroom. He is needed in our homes. The alternative is despair, hopelessness, and emptiness.

I learned that stewardship is not just about money. It's about life. We need a holistic view of stewardship that involves all the facets of our lives. Stewardship of our financial capital is part of it, but the stewardship of our relational capital, our family and friends, is another. We must also be stewards of our intellectual capital, our human capital, and our spiritual capital. All those elements of our lives must function in harmony.

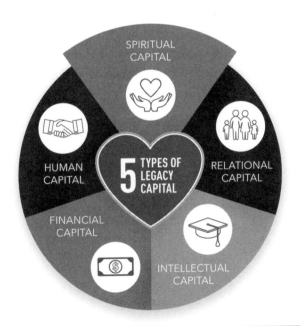

In his book *Halftime*, Bob Buford described his journey "from success to significance," and his Halftime Institute helps people to gain clarity about their life purpose. Success alone will not satisfy. Money and stuff is not enough. If that's all you have, you eventually feel the emptiness. We each need in some way to feel that we are significant, that we are here for a reason.

King Solomon, in Ecclesiastes 5:10–15 (NIV), warned of the unsatisfying pursuit of money and things:

Whoever loves money never has enough; whoever loves wealth is never satisfied with their income. This too is meaningless. As goods increase, so do those who consume them. And what benefit are they to the owners except to feast their eyes on them? The sleep of a laborer is sweet, whether they eat little or much, but as for the rich, their abundance permits them no sleep. I have seen a grievous evil under the sun: wealth hoarded to the harm of its owners, or wealth lost through some misfortune, so that when they have children there is nothing left for them to inherit. Everyone comes naked from their mother's womb, and as everyone comes, so they depart. They take nothing from their toil that they can carry in their hands.

As Rabbi Harold Kusher, put it: "No one ever said on their deathbed: "I wish I had spent more time at the office." We need to make what matters most our top priority, our relationship with God through Jesus Christ, and our relationships with family and friends and those whom God has put in our sphere of influence. These matter infinitely more than the money and the stuff.

___

If you want to build an enduring legacy, it can't just be a legacy for a lifetime, or even for multiple generations. It needs to be everlasting. And the only way to have an eternal legacy is to have an eternal destiny and relationship with the God of the universe through Jesus Christ. Are you prepared for eternity? If today were your last day and you had to stand before Almighty God, what would you say to Him if He asked why you should be allowed into heaven?

True contentment cannot be found in materialism. Along with attaining financial freedom, we need a spirit of generosity. Howard Dayton, who is the cofounder with Larry Burkett of Crown Financial Ministries, and whose new ministry is Compass—Finances God's Way, has said that "money is a chief competitor for the lordship of Christ over our lives." We must not let money rule us. To live out a successful legacy, we need financial freedom instead of bondage, and we need faith instead of fear. We need to live our lives faithfully and through the lens of eternity.

SETTING OUR SIGHTS ON ETERNITY

I leave you with a few questions to consider as you build your personal, family, financial, business, and Kingdom legacies.

- What are the things that matter most to you?

- Who are the top ten people in the world you care most about? Do they know how you feel about them? How might you invest in each of them?

- Is there anything that has been left unsaid that one day you will wish you had said? What are those words, and who needs to hear them?

- Have you created a list of things to accomplish while you still have time? (Call it a bucket list with an eternal perspective!)

- Do you have an intentional plan, one that is more than wishful thinking, to live and leave a lasting personal and family legacy?

- Do you have an intentional, proactive, and written plan to prepare and mentor your children and grandchildren by transferring wisdom, family values, virtues, life lessons, and life stories to them? Do you have a plan for effective wealth transfer combined with intentional wisdom transfer?

- If you are a business owner, how are you preparing the next generation of leaders to steward your business legacy?

Those questions, and many similar ones, focus on the importance of incorporating wisdom transfer into your legacy plans. Most plans focus only on transferring the wealth, leaving out what is most important. I would submit to you that when it comes to leaving a legacy for your children or grandchildren, if you had to make a choice between leaving them wealth or leaving them wisdom, you would be better off leaving them wisdom. If they have wisdom, they can create their own wealth.

The good news is it's not a zero-sum game. You do not have to make that choice. You can leave them both wealth and wisdom. If that is to happen, however, you need to carefully plan so that you are preparing the rising generations to become wise stewards. You need to instill in them the virtues, character, values, and work ethic that you know will engender true success, fending off the spirit of entitlement and the affliction of affluenza. Today, through your intercession and compassion, you can help to prepare your heirs for their rightful role in eternity. By passing down wisdom

> Only one life, 'twill soon be past / Only what's done for Christ will last.

along with wealth, you can help them to become the type of people God wants them to be.

Let us set our sights on eternity. As the British missionary C. T. Studd wrote in a moment of poetic inspiration: "Only one life, 'twill soon be past / Only what's done for Christ will last." That is the essence of building a legacy that truly will endure.

EPILOGUE

GOODBYE TO GRAM

In May 1999, Gram Rogers went home to be with the Lord. My father and other family members asked me to preach at her funeral in a small church in Ossipee, New Hampshire.

The day was bittersweet, almost surreal in its mixture of pain and peace, of loss and love. We felt pangs of sorrow over her passing from our presence, but we felt abounding joy in knowing absolutely where she had gone. She was in heaven, in the presence of Jesus. This was something to celebrate, as was the life she had lived and the legacy she left behind. During the service, one of my aunts stepped out in faith, and it was my stepmom and spiritual mom who led her to Christ that day.

I had the opportunity as I spoke that day to reflect on the many lives that Gram had touched: the farm families to whom she brought groceries, her business clients, her friends and neighbors, and my family and me.

There are a lot of wealthy people in this world who lack wisdom. Their money brings them no lasting joy. Their happiness is superficial. Other people have wisdom without a lot of wealth. Gram was one of those souls. She had made good money and could have kept it for herself, but she chose to live with open hands and an open heart to meet the needs of others. As she gave of her wealth, she met people's needs in practical ways. She served as the hands, feet, and heart of Jesus. She loved Him with all her heart, and she loved others, and that led her to serve. And when she smiled, it was Jesus's smile on the world.

Gram gave freely of her wisdom, as well. I am eternally grateful for the lessons that she taught me, and in turn, my quest is to do my best to share that wisdom with others. Her example showed me that we need to be Christ centered and others oriented. Hers was the spirit of generosity. She believed our focus should not be merely to lay up our treasure here on earth, where moths and rust and thieves may destroy it, but rather, to lay up our treasure in heaven where it will endure for all eternity. That is how she lived, and that is the wisdom and example she left as part of her legacy.

Wisdom and wealth are not at all mutually exclusive. You can have both. Whether you have been blessed with a modest sum or significant affluence, your challenge is to steward it well. And as God has made you rich in wisdom as well, you can pass it on to your children and grandchildren and those in your spheres of influence. These are the virtues, the values, and the life lessons that are worthy of preserving for all time. These are the reflection of your character.

It was my privilege to walk with Gram Rogers for a while. I close my eyes and once again I am a boy traveling through the countryside with her as she served the needy. She dedicated herself to planting seeds in others, and, as I finally recognized, in me. She lived out her faith like a beacon, and as a youth, I knew that she was genuine, even as I was stumbling in the dark, trying to find my own godless way. I saw in Gram Rogers no sign of the hypocrisy that sometimes alienates young people from their parents, grandparents, and the church. I know that she kept me in prayer, and I know that her faith had much to do with how I found my faith—and my calling.

I think back to that day when she gave me my first Bible and showed me where I could find my refuge and strength. I ask you now: Have you put your faith in Jesus Christ? Is He your refuge and strength? If so, will you, too, be a beacon of light and hope to a lost and dying and hurting world that desperately needs hope and the Good News of Jesus Christ? Will you be a faithful ambassador of the King of Kings?

You have the opportunity to write your own legacy and that of your family and your business. Write it well! Write it in the spirit of Gram Rogers, from whose life I learned this: if you have wealth but you don't have wisdom, you don't have much.

If this book has been a blessing to you, we would encourage you to share it with others. Give it as a gift, tell others about it, talk about it on social media, or write a review on Amazon. Additionally, if you feel you would benefit by having a guide to help you, your spouse, and your family to navigate the answers to the questions raised in this book or to create a family or business legacy plan, please contact us. We're here to help and we would love to serve you and help you to build a thriving family legacy!

APPENDIX

THRIVING FAMILY LEGACY ASSESSMENT

Name _____   Date _____

	1	2	3	4	5	
I/we cannot clearly envision or communicate the family legacy we would like to create.						I/we can clearly envision and communicate the family legacy we would like to create.
I/we are not 100 percent confident that all our children and grand-children would still be "hugging each other" six months after we died.						I/we are 100 percent confident that all our children and grand-children would still be "hugging each other" six months after we died.
We do not have a well-defined (and written) Family Vision, Mission, and Core Values statement.						We have a well-defined (and written) Family Vision, Mission, and Core Values statement.
Some of our children or grandchildren are not fully prepared to be wise stewards of the wealth they might inherit.						All of our children or grandchildren are fully prepared to be wise stewards of the wealth they might inherit.
My spouse and I are not completely in alignment in our vision for our children and grandchil-dren and our Family Legacy.						My spouse and I are completely in alignment in our vision for our children and grandchil-dren and our Family Legacy.

We do not have an intentional, proactive, and written plan that includes both Wisdom Transfer and Wealth Transfer to our children and grandchildren.						We do have an intentional, proactive, and written plan that includes both Wisdom Transfer and Wealth Transfer to our children and grandchildren.
I/we do not feel a sense of true financial freedom.						Both my spouse and I feel a complete sense of true financial freedom.
I believe conflicts and/or unresolved issues exist in my family that interferes with building a Thriving Family Legacy.						I believe there are no conflicts and/or unresolved issues in my family that might interfere with building a Thriving Family Legacy.
I am not 100 percent sure if we have a Zero Estate and IRD Tax Plan.						I am 100 percent sure if we have a Zero Estate and IRD Tax Plan.
If I passed away right now, I would have some regrets over things I would have left "unsaid" to my spouse, children, grandparents, parents, or others.						If I passed away right now, I would not have any regrets over things I would have left "unsaid" to my spouse, children, grandparents, parents, or others.
If I stepped into eternity today, I am not confident I would get a "hug" and hear "Well done!" from God the Father.						If I stepped into eternity today, I am confident I would get a "hug" and hear "Well done!" from my heavenly Father.
Add column Totals						Your Score_____

RESOURCES

Many of those who are reading this book are already members of the family of Christian faith. If not, let me suggest some resources that can help you, too, put your faith and trust in Jesus Christ and surrender your life to Him.

Holy Bible (John 3:16–17, John 10:10b, Romans 3:23, Romans 6:23, Romans 8: 1, Ephesians 2:8–10).

Campus Crusade for Christ. *The Four Spiritual Laws* (booklet originally written by the late Dr. Bill Bright).

The Navigators. *The Bridge.* A gospel video. https://www.navigators.org/resource/the-bridge-to-life/.

Alcorn, Randy. *Money, Possessions and Eternity.* Carol Stream: Tyndale House Publishers, 2013.

Alcorn, Randy. *The Treasure Principle: Unlocking the Secret of Joyful Giving.* New York: Multnomah Books, 2005.

Blue, Ron. *Splitting Heirs: Giving Your Money and Things to Your Children without Ruining Their Lives.* Chicago: Northfield Publishing, 2008.

Ron Blue is the founding director of Kingdom Advisors.

Buford, Bob. *Halftime: Moving from Success to Significance.* With a foreword by Jim Collins. New York: Zondervan, 2015.

Bob Buford describes the journey "from success to significance."

Buford, Bob. *Halftime for Couples.* Irving: Halftime Institute.

Cochell, Perry and Rod Zeeb. *Beating the Midas Curse.* Jackson: Allegiance Publishing, 2013.

Conway, Tom, Lori Coonan, Todd DeKruyter et al. *unPrepared: Heirs at Risk: 14 Elements for Successful Wealth Transfer.* Jeff Rogers contributed to this publication. Indianapolis: The Center for Family Conversations (now Family Meridian), 2017.

Dayton, Howard. *Charting Your Legacy.* Orlando: Compass—Finances God's Way, 2018.

Dayton, Howard. *Money and Marriage God's Way.* Chicago: Moody Publishers, 2009.

DeKruyter, Todd, *Navigating Life with more than Enough.* Sarasota: Weaver Crosspoint.

Dobson, James. Focus on the Family. https://www.focusonthefamily.com/media/focus-on-the-family-commentary/strong-willed-child. Dr. Dobson comments on how to raise a strong-willed child.

Green, David. *Giving It All Away ... and Getting It All Back Again.* New York: Zondervan, 2017.

David Green is the founder of Hobby Lobby.

Greer, Peter. *Mission Drift: The Unspoken Crisis Facing Leaders, Charities, and Churches.* Ada: Bethany House Publishers, 2015.

Karcher, Bob and Susan Karcher. *Who Are the Joneses Anyway? Stop Living Someone Else's Life and Start Becoming Who You Are Meant to Be.* New York: Morgan James Publishing, 2016.

LeTourneau, R. G. *Mover of Men and Mountains.* Chicago: Moody Publishers, 1967.

Morley, Patrick. *The Man in the Mirror.* New York: Zondervan, 2014.

MyVerge. *The Missional Family.* my.vergenetwork.org.

This e-book offers simple ways to live out the gospel in everyday family life.

Niewolny, Dean. *Trade Up: How to Move from Just Making Money to Making a Difference*. With a foreword by Bob Buford. Ada: Baker Books, 2017.

O'Neil, Jessie. *The Golden Ghetto: The Psychology of Affluence*. Affluenza Project, 1997.

O'Neil describes the scourge of "affluenza."

Reeb, Lloyd and Bob Buford. *From Success to Significance: When the Pursuit of Success Isn't Enough*. New York: Zondervan, 2018.

Spadafora, Jeff. *The Joy Model: A Step-by-Step Guide to Peace, Purpose, and Balance*. New York: Thomas Nelson, 2016.

Tam, Stanley. *God Owns My Business*. Chicago: WingSpread Publishers, 2013.

Warren, Rick. *The Purpose Driven Life: What on Earth Am I Here For?* New York: Zondervan, 2013.

York, David and Andrew Howell. *Entrusted: Building a Legacy That Lasts*. YH Publishing, 2015.

Resources for Christian Business Owners

Thriving Business Legacy: www.StewardshipLegacy.com\ThrivingBusiness

C12 Group (Christian Business Owner & CEO Roundtable Group): www.C12Group.com

Convene: www.convenenow.com

Fellowship of Companies for Christ International: www.fcci.org

Resources for Charitable Giving, Donor-Advised Funds, and Foundation Resources

The Signatry—A Global Christian Foundation: www.thesignatry.com

National Christian Foundation: www.ncfgiving.com

WaterStone: www.waterstone.org

The Orchard Foundation: https://www.theorchard.org

Resources for "What's next?" in the Second Half of Life

The Halftime Institute: www.Halftime.org

The Way: www.theway2life.org

www.stewardshiplegacy.com/resources

www.stewardshiplegacy.com/business

ABOUT THE AUTHOR

Jeff Rogers is the ForbesBooks featured author of *Create a Thriving Family Legacy: How to Share your Wisdom and Wealth with Your Children and Grandchildren*, the co-author of *unPrepared: Heirs at Risk: 14 Elements for Successful Wealth Transfer* and author of the e-book, *The Stewardship of Your Business Legacy ... Wisely Stewarding the Largest Financial Transaction of Your Life ... Without Getting Killed with Taxes*. He is the Founder of Stewardship Legacy Coaching. In 2013, Jeff was the recipient of the Larry Burkett Award from Kingdom Advisors, their highest award. He has over thirty-five years of experience in Zero Estate Tax Planning and Multi-Generational Family Legacy Coaching. Jeff is nationally recognized for his expertise in Strategic and Tactical Tax Planning and Charitable Planning. Jeff assists high-net-worth individuals and business owners in creating "Kingdom Capital™" by redirecting tax dollars to their favorite ministries.

5 AREAS OF YOUR LEGACY

| PERSONAL | FAMILY | FINANCIAL | BUSINESS | KINGDOM |
| Legacy | Legacy | Legacy | Legacy | Legacy |

WHAT IS STEWARDSHIP LEGACY COACHING?

Stewardship Legacy Coaching™ extends beyond the dollar sign to help you accumulate lasting treasure and leave a lasting legacy. It is a unique process we use to assist our clients in the following five areas of their Legacy™.

WHAT KIND OF LEGACY WILL YOU LEAVE?

PERSONAL

Gain enhanced clarity concerning:

- Your unique, God-given Life Purpose.

- Going from "Success" to "Significance."

- The fulfillment of your mission for the "second half" of your life.

- Optimization of the use of your time, talents, and treasures, as well as your leadership and influence, so as to positively impact the lives of others, especially family members, while considering and implementing plans that impact the Kingdom of God.

FAMILY

Become proactive and intentional about:

- Intergenerational mentoring of our children and grandchildren.

- Passing on virtues and values as part of our legacy.

- Intergenerational reconciliation (if needed).

- Passing on Wisdom as well as Wealth.

- Passing on our faith, a heart for ministry and a passion for generosity to our heirs.

FINANCIAL

Gain enhanced confidence as you consider and answer these questions:

- How much is enough for us?

- How much is enough for our children and grandchildren?

- What is an appropriate inheritance (so that it is a blessing and not a curse)?

- How do we structure their inheritance to protect it for them and protect it from them?

- How can we train our family members to be wise stewards of their inheritance?

- How can I prepare my spouse to make wise financial decisions after I'm gone?

- How can I create a Zero Estate and IRD Tax Plan?

- How do I save significant money in current income and/ or capital gains taxes?

- How can I convert my "Social Capital" (taxes) to Kingdom Capital to help fund the Great Commission?

BUSINESS

Become wise stewards of your business legacy by:

- Seeing God as the Owner of our business and ourselves as His "Chief Stewardship Officers."

- Casting a vision for the future of the business and effectively communicating the mission and values throughout the organization.

- Training the next generation of business stewards and leaders.

- Prudent Business Succession and Exit Planning.

- Integrating your faith throughout your business.

- Becoming intentional and proactive about stewarding your business culture.

- Using your business as a platform of influence to your employees, clients, customers, vendors, and the community at large.

- Using your business as a conduit for Kingdom Capital (and saving taxes in the process!).

KINGDOM

Increase your personal and financial
IMPACT on ETERNITY by:

- Casting a ministry vision based on your ministry passions.

- Investing your time, talents, treasures, leadership, relationships, and influence in the Kingdom.

- Involving children and/or grandchildren in our giving and modeling Biblical Stewardship and generosity to them.